Surviving Fighter Aircraft of World War Two

Surviving Fighter Aircraft of World War Two

A Global Guide to Location and Types

Don Berliner

Pen & Sword
AVIATION

First published in Great Britain in 2011 by
Pen & Sword Aviation
An imprint of
Pen & Sword Books Ltd
47 Church Street
Barnsley
South Yorkshire
S70 2AS

ISBN 978 1 84884 265 6

Typeset in 10.5pt Palatino by Mac Style, Beverley, East Yorkshire
Printed and bound in India by Replika Press Pvt. Ltd.

Pen & Sword Books Ltd incorporates the Imprints of Pen & Sword Aviation, Pen & Sword
Family History, Pen & Sword Maritime, Pen & Sword Military, Pen & Sword Discovery,
Wharncliffe Local History, Wharncliffe True Crime, Wharncliffe Transport, Pen & Sword Select,
Pen & Sword Military Classics, Leo Cooper, The Praetorian Press, Remember When,
Seaforth Publishing and Frontline Publishing

For a complete list of Pen & Sword titles please contact
PEN & SWORD BOOKS LIMITED
47 Church Street, Barnsley, South Yorkshire, S70 2AS, England
E-mail: enquiries@pen-and-sword.co.uk
Website: www.pen-and-sword.co.uk

Contents

Introduction

A million and a half aircraft have been built since the Wright Brothers presented the world with their 1903 Flyer that achieved what earlier, so-called airplanes did not: FLIGHT! Most have been airplanes (fixed-wing, powered, heavier-than-air, man-carrying), but many others were seaplanes, gliders, helicopters and lighter-than-air blimps and dirigibles.

Almost half of all those 1,500,000 aircraft were built for World War Two: 750,000 fighters, bombers, transports, trainers, scouts, gliders and helicopters. Most were built in the United States, Great Britain, France, the Soviet Union, Czechoslovakia, Canada, Australia, the Netherlands, Finland, Poland, Germany, Japan, Italy, and Spain.

The total includes older aircraft that remained in military service at the start of World War Two, all those built during and for the war, and all those flown prior to V-J Day on 15 August 1945, even if only in the form of a single prototype that did not get into production before the war ended.

For the purpose of this book, a 'basic type' is exemplified by the P-51 Mustang, while the P-51A and P-51B are considered 'sub-types'. Of more than 500 basic types built as production designs or unsuccessful prototypes, 60 per cent still exist in at least one example and most of them have been restored to near-new (sometimes better than new) condition. Sadly, the remaining 40 per cent seem to have disappeared for good, though hardly

any of those can be considered major types. And there is still the remote chance that one or more of them may be discovered in a remote barn or some vast scrap yard.

The total of individual surviving World War Two aircraft is well over four thousand. Easily the most popular type is the North American AT-6/SNJ/Harvard advanced trainer, with almost 1,300 known to exist in some recognizable condition. A significant proportion are not only flyable, but regularly flown as warbirds. The most common sub-types are the AT-6G with 290 survivors, the AT-6D with 270, and the SNJ-4 with 160.

Of the fighters, there are close to 1,000 known, with the P-51 the most popular, at 340 examples, its P-51D sub-type accounting for 275. There are about 220 Spitfires, of which the Mk.IX accounts for 60 and the Mk.XVI, 40.

When completed, this three-volume series will cover about 330 basic types and 500 basic and sub-types combined. Roughly half of them are the only known example to survive for 65 years.

This first volume covers fighters (also known in the US as 'pursuits'). As World War Two was becoming inevitable, most air forces were still equipped with squadrons of open-cockpit pursuit biplanes having fixed landing gears and piston engines, and at least partially covered with doped fabric. Few had top speeds exceeding 250mph. When the war ended, the main air powers – the United States, Great Britain, Germany – were building scientifically-designed airplanes powered by turbojet engines that could easily top 500mph and sometimes approach 600mph.

The second volume will concentrate on bombers, with about 80 basic types known to exist. The final volume will show all the other types, with at least 150 transports, trainers, rotary-wing, gliders, seaplanes, scout and reconnaissance, research and record-setting and miscellaneous craft.

In all three volumes the author has been faced with the problem of dealing with multi-purpose airplanes such as fighter-bombers, scout-bombers, liaison/utility planes and training gliders. Rather than list them in both categories, he has chosen to list each by its primary function, with reference to the other(s). Even so, some designs simply refuse to be categorized, creating a need for a 'miscellaneous' category.

Chapter One
US Army

Boeing P-26 Peashooter

The sprightly little P-26 was a short-lived bridge between the seat-of-the-pants past and the technological future. It combined wire bracing for the wings, an open cockpit and fixed landing gear, with all-metal construction and monoplane design. It was the first such modern airplane ordered by either the US Army or US Navy, yet was strongly opposed by those who insisted that a pilot must feel the air in order to fly, and who rejected retractable landing gear as too heavy and too unreliable, and a single wing without external bracing as simply not safe.

Boeing entered the pursuit business in 1923 with the PW-9, a conventional biplane powered by a 435hp Curtiss liquid-cooled V-12 engine, and which won contracts from the Army for 110 airplanes, and from the Navy (as the FB-1) for 14 more. Having established itself as a major manufacturer, Boeing added to its reputation in 1929 with the first contract for what would become the standard pursuit for both the Army (P-12) and Navy (F4B), both using the popular 450hp Pratt & Whitney R-1340 Wasp radial engine.

While it was still building P-12s and F4Bs, Boeing prepared to move into the future with an all-metal monoplane. The firm's horizons had been expanded to include development of commercial and multi-engined military airplanes, which may have given it the courage to re-enter the pursuit business with a somewhat radical design.

The prototype P-26 first flew on 20 March 1932, and made everything else then being flown by the US military look decidedly old fashioned. Gone was the top wing, along with its interplane struts. While the landing gear was still fixed, it was carefully streamlined. It looked faster than even the sleekest of biplanes, and in fact had a higher top speed as well as a higher landing speed. Criticism of the latter led to the first set of camber-increasing wing flaps installed on any production Army airplane.

Compared with the then-standard Boeing biplane pursuits, the new P-26 was more than 40mph faster and could fly almost 100 miles further on its internal fuel load. Due to its higher wing-loading, compared with the P-12 it had a reduced rate of climb and maximum altitude. Generals and pilots complained, but the future won out, and 139 were ordered in an era when the military's conservatism was accentuated by the Great Depression and ensuing lack of funds.

Of the total built, 111 were P-26As. Twenty-five P-26Bs were then ordered with a more powerful, fuel-injected Wasp engine, but as Pratt & Whitney was unable to deliver on time, they became

P-26Cs, which were then gradually re-equipped with the better engine. The P-26 became the Army's standard pursuit plane, and from then on, no biplane fighter was bought by the Army.

With the P-26 showing the way to the future, other manufacturers jumped on the monoplane bandwagon, with the result that the Peashooter was soon rendered obsolete. Boeing tried to regain its position with a highly cleaned-up version called the P-29, but as it offered too little increase in speed, it died on the vine.

The US never used the P-26 in combat, most of them having been retired to the less glamorous jobs of training pilots and mechanics before 7 December 1941, when the Japanese attack on Pearl Harbor catapulted an officially neutral nation into all-out war. A few were still on active duty in the Panama Canal Zone at the start of the war, but were soon replaced by more modern airplanes which stood by to repulse Japanese attacks which never occurred.

A few had been sold to China and were flown with surprising success against the Japanese in 1937, after which they were replaced by British Gloster Gladiator biplanes. The only post-Pearl Harbor action for the P-26 was in the hands of Philippine Army Air Corps pilots, who threw their last remaining Boeings into the air in a hopeless attempt to counter the waves of Japanese fighters and bombers attacking Manila and surrounding targets. The last recorded aerial combat was on 23 December when a P-26 managed to shoot down a Zero. The few that were left were burned a few days later to keep them from falling into enemy hands, though it is hard to imagine that the Japanese would have had much interest in some obsolete fighters.

The P-26 was the last American fighter with an open cockpit and non-retractable landing gear, as well as the last fighter designed and produced solely by Boeing. Only two of the original 139 are known to have survived.

Specifications of the P-26A

Length: 23ft 10in
Wingspan: 27ft 11in
Height: 10ft 5in
Maximum speed: 227mph
Maximum range: 360 miles
Rate of climb: 2,360ft/min
Service ceiling: 27,400ft

Surviving Examples

P-26A
USAAC 33-123 – Planes of Fame
USAAC 33-135 – US National Air & Space Museum

Seversky P-35

The Seversky Aircraft Corp. was founded in 1931 by Russian émigré Alexander P de Seversky with money he received from selling an improved bombsight to the US Government. His immediate goal was to design and produce modern fighter planes.

His first successful American design was the SEV-3M, a sleek amphibian that flew in 1933. He soon settled on his basic plan, turning out prototype military airplanes and sport versions in which Jackie Cochran and Frank Fuller won the last three pre-war Bendix Transcontinental Derbies from Los Angeles to Cleveland. They brought de Seversky considerable public acclaim, along with serious attention from the military.

The first serious attempt at a Seversky fighter was the model SEV-2XP, a two-place pursuit with fixed landing gear. Following an accident, it was converted into a single-place airplane with

retractable landing gear, but its 850hp Wright R-1820 Cyclone engine lacked the power to enable it to reach 300mph. A Pratt & Whitney R-1830 engine and other changes still could not get it to the speed required by the US Army Air Corps.

Finally, with yet more changes, Seversky was awarded a contract for 77 examples of what had by then been designated the P-35. Deliveries began in July 1937, and were completed in August 1938, of an airplane that could reach 281mph and an altitude of 30,600 feet. It carried one .30 cal. and one .50 cal. machine gun, which seemed to be sufficient firepower for peacetime.

The Army Air Corps' final Seversky P-35 became the Republic XP-41 when it received inward-retracting landing gear and a supercharged P&W R-1340 engine, giving it a top speed of 323mph, However, the Army found the high-altitude version of the P-35, which it called the XP-43 Lancer, even more interesting.

In June 1939, Sweden ordered a total of 120 of the export version of the P-35, designated the EP-106. Half the Swedish order was held back for the US Army Air Corps, and most of those were sent to units in the Phillipines, where they provided much of the defense when the Japanese attacked in December 1941. With a top speed of barely over 300mph, and only four machine guns, they were badly out-classed, and the few that remained were destroyed to keep them from being captured.

Specifications of the P-35A

Length: 26ft 10in
Wingspan: 36ft 0in
Height: 9ft 9in
Wing area: 220 sq ft
Maximum speed: 310mph at 14,300ft

Maximum range: 600 miles at 260mph
Service ceiling: 31,400ft
Rate of climb: 1,920ft/min

Surviving Examples include:

P-35A

USAAC 282-11 – National Museum of the US Air Force
USAAC 262-11 – Fantasy of Flight

EP-106

c/n 2134 – Swedish Air Force Museum

2PA

c/n 483-38 – Planes of Fame

Curtiss P-36 Hawk

What eventually became the Curtiss-Wright Corporation was well established as a supplier of airplanes to the US Army and US Navy, starting as far back as 1911, when a Curtiss Model D became the Army's second airplane. Subsequently, Curtiss produced thousands of JN-4 'Jenny' trainers during World War One, and many types of Hawk biplane pursuits for both services through the mid-1930s.

Curtiss built the prototype of its P-36 Hawk pursuit as the Y1P-36, which flew in March 1937, as the company's first all-metal, low-wing airplane with retractable-landing gear. With a top speed of 295mph at 20,000 feet on the power of a 900hp Pratt & Whitney R-1830 Twin Wasp radial engine, it impressed the Army sufficiently to warrant an unusually large order (for the time) for 210 P-36As by July 1937.

The new Hawk became the basis for extensive experimental modifications, from the XP-36B through to the XP-36F, with various combinations of engines and machine guns. None of these entered production, but other ideas led directly to the Curtiss XP-37 and the XP-42, both of which had long pointed cowlings around their radial engines that made them appear like enclosed in-line engines. These machines, too, failed to be rewarded with production contracts, which eventually went to the P-40, which was basically a P-36 with a V-12 Allison V-1710 engine.

The variation on the basic P-36 that became the most popular was the Hawk 75, the export version. The 75 was a P-36 with fixed, streamlined landing gear, and an 875hp Wright GR-1820 engine. It was bought by China (113), Thailand (75) and Argentina (30 built by Curtiss, 200 built in Argentina on license).

Of more interest to other countries was the Hawk 75A with retractable landing gear, and either a 1,200hp Pratt & Whitney R-1830 engine or Wright R-1820 Cyclone of similar power. They had either one or three .30 cal. and one .50 cal. machine guns. 75As were bought by France (291 delivered and 304 diverted to other countries when France fell to the Nazi invasion). Finland bought 44, Norway 48, all of which were seized by the US before delivery and later sent to Peru and to the Norwegian air-force-in-exile training base in Canada. Great Britain received 227 originally meant for France, and sent them to India and South Africa. Portugal, Iran and the Netherlands also received small numbers of the 1,000+ Hawk 75s that came off the assembly lines. Clearly, the Hawk 75 was seen as a fighter suited to minor air forces.

The combat record of the P-36 and Hawk 75 was a very mixed bag, with some history made along the way. Though considered obsolete by the US Army Air Corps, two squadrons were at Pearl Harbor on 7 December 1941 and scored a few successes. A short period of service with the Army Reserves followed, with the the the P-36s' American career ending with them being used in training.

France, with the largest number of Hawk 75As, threw them into battles against much newer German airplanes. They were credited with France's first aerial victories of the war, and eventually with more than 200 enemy planes destroyed and another 80 damaged.

Specifications of the P-36C/Hawk 75A

Length: 28ft 6in
Wingspan: 37ft 4in
Height: 9ft 6in
Wing area: 236 sq ft

Maximum speed: 311mph at 10,000ft
Maximum range: 820 miles at 200mph
Service ceiling: 33,700ft

Surviving Examples

P-36A
USAAC 38-001 – National Museum of the US Air Force

Hawk 75A-1
USAAC '82' – Imperial War Museum (Duxford)

Lockheed P-38 Lightning

It was a radical idea from the lively imagination of Hal Hibbard's design team, which included young Clarence 'Kelly' Johnson, later to be recognized as one of history's great designers. In response to a US Army Air Corps requirement for a 400mph interceptor, they created a twin-engined, twin-boom machine that surprised everyone by reaching 400mph on one of its first flights. Lockheed reasoned that the only way to have an interceptor with the required performance was to use two engines, as no existing single engine had sufficient power.

The only remotely similar American machine at that time was Bell's YFM-1 Airacuda, a prototype escort fighter that was the size of a medium bomber, carried a five-man crew and could not reach 300mph.

The prototype XP-38 first flew on 27 January 1939, the first American fighter with tricycle landing gear. Six weeks later, 13 YP-38 service test airplanes were ordered, followed in August by an order for 66 production P-38s. Power was a pair of Allison

V-12 V-1710 engines turning in opposite directions to cancel out the effects of propeller torque. Armament originally consisted of a single 37mm cannon, two .30 cal. and two .50 cal. machine guns, all mounted in the nose of the pilot's nacelle and firing straight ahead.

Major orders soon followed: 667 for an export version, 607 more for the US Army. Even though the YP-38 had shown its ability to hit 407mph at 20,000 feet after a six-minute dash to that altitude, the assembly line was slow in developing. Finally, the P-38D became the first true production version, with the first of them getting to squadrons in August 1941, followed closely by the P-38E with a 20mm cannon in lieu of the 37mm. Almost half the order of 210 became F-4 photo-reconnaissance versions.

The Lightning's introduction into the war in Europe was delayed by the RAF insisting on a change to propellers that turned in the same direction, and the removal of the turbo-superchargers. This was done, and the predictable drop in performance led to all the airplanes being rejected by the RAF. The USAAF also had problems, with many of its fighter pilots hesitant to go into combat with something as radical as a twin, until Lockheed test pilot Tony LeVier demonstrated its ability to operate on a single engine, with an air show routine that was later copied to great acclaim by Bob Hoover in a P-51D Mustang.

Production rapidly increased, as did the power of the twin Allison engines. The brief consideration of switching to Rolls-Royce Merlin engines was discarded when it became clear that the production Merlins was already scheduled for other airplanes. Along with this came the development of the P-38 into the most versatile American fighter of the war, being adaptable to night fighting, bombing (with up to 4,000lb of bombs slung under the wings), and also being used as a high-altitude escort fighter. With

the P-38M, a night fighter with radar, operated by a smallish man crammed into the severely limited space behind the pilot.

Two follow-on airplanes were developed by Lockheed during the war: the XP-49 with two 1,600hp Continental inverted V-12 engines and a pressurized cockpit, and the XP-58 Chain Lightning which was a large (70ft wingspan, 31,000lb empty weight) bomber destroyer powered by two Allison double-V-12 engines, in the same class as Northrop's P-61 Black Widow. Neither of these projects got beyond prototype stage, as Lockheed was poised to charge into the jet age, which it did with great success.

Specifications of the P-38L

Length: 37ft 10in
Wingspan: 52ft 0in
Height: 9ft 10in
Wing area: 328 sq ft
Maximum speed: 414mph at 25,000ft
Maximum range: 2,260 miles at 185mph with two 300-gallon drop tanks
Service ceiling: 44,000ft
Rate of climb: 20,000ft in 5:00

Surviving Examples

P-38E
USAAF 42-12652 – Flying Heritage Collection

P-38F
USAAF 41-7630 – 'Glacier Girl' recovered from Greenland

P-38G
USAAF 42-13400 – Elmendorf AFB

large droppable fuel tanks, later models could be ferried directly across the Atlantic.

It was in the Pacific that the airplane came into its own, with its pilots shooting down more Japanese airplanes than pilots of any other type, Army or Navy. The most striking example of the P-38's long-range interception ability was the downing, after a long over-water flight, of a Japanese 'Betty' bomber carrying Admiral Yamamoto, one of the architects of the attack on Pearl Harbor. America's all-time top ace – Richard Bong – got all 40 of his victories in P-38s, as did runner-up Thomas McGuire, with 38.

The most common version was the P-38L, with 1,475hp engines and mountings for ten 5in rockets under the wings. Almost 4,000 were built, out of a total of almost 9,400. At the end of the war, orders for another 1,887 were cancelled. The final version was

P-38H
USAAF 42-66841 – Classic Fighter Jets Museum

P-38J
USAAF 42-67638 – Hill AFB
USAAF 42-67762 – US National Air & Space Museum
USAAF 42-23314 – Planes of Fame

P-38L
USAAF 44-26761 – Fantasy of Flight
USAAF 44-53015 – McGuire AFB
USAAF 44-53232 – National Museum of the US Air Force
USAAF 44-53087 – EAA Museum

About 35 more, mainly in American museums

Bell P-39 Airacobra

The P-39 was proposed as a dogfighter, failed at this, and then became an excellent close support tank-buster.

Bell was incorporated in 1936 and built its first airplane – the twin-pusher XFM-1 Airacuda – in 1938. While 13 were built, the Airacuda's performance was not up to scratch and it was not put into production. The next airplane from the Buffalo, NY, manufacturer bore no similarity to its first, though it did include some novel ideas. The engine was a low-altitude version of the Allison V-1710 V-12, located behind the pilot and driving a three-bladed propeller via a long drive shaft. It was hoped that this concentration of weight near the center of the airplane would result in better maneuverability, but it didn't turn out this way. In fact, it gave the Airacobra poor spin recovery characteristics.

Other ideas tried on the prototype were a side-opening door like that on an automobile, and a tricycle landing gear. While the door

BELL P-39 AIRACOBRA
B.F.GOODRICH DE-ICERS.

actually made bailing out somewhat more difficult and dangerous, the nose wheel-style landing gear made for much better handling during landing and take off, especially in crosswinds.

The XP-39 made its first flight in April 1939, and soon recorded a surprising top speed of 390mph at 20,000 feet, thanks to a very well streamlined airframe, and a take-off weight well under what was expected for the production version. By the time the P-39D began rolling off the lines, it had grown heavier by 2,000lb, though a reduction in wingspan had improved its ability to turn tightly, at the cost of extending the take-off and landing distances.

The next version was at first called the P-45, but was re-designated the P-39C as it varied little from the P-39D.

The first deliveries to AAF squadrons came in February 1941. Along with this came an order for 675 Airacobra Is for the RAF, these differing from the P-39D mainly in the replacement of the 37mm cannon by one of only 20mm. Tests by the British revealed enough deficiencies in speed, take-off run and operational ceiling to warrant rejecting the entire order, many of them ending up in the USSR.

Airacobras were sent to USAAF units in the Southwest Pacific, but were no match for the highly maneuverable Japanese fighters. Others were used more effectively in North Africa for ground support. Production was accelerated, with more than 2,000 P-39Ns being built, having slightly improved performance due to the elimination of some internal fuel tanks and even some armor plating. The P-39Q became the most common type, with almost 5,000 built.

The Airacobra was a public success, thanks to its very modern, almost sporty look. It quickly became a favorite with aeromodellers, but unfortunately not with its pilots. The relatively poor speed, maneuverability and high-altitude performance made it inferior

to other American and foreign fighters of the day. As a result, the USAAF offered it to the USSR, which was in desperate need of almost anything that would fly. Of 9,500 built, 4,700 were shipped directly to the Red Air Force, which recognized the P-39's qualities in the ground support role. It could withstand considerable battle damage, and could attack German tanks with great effectiveness with its 37mm nose-mounted cannon.

A US Navy version of the Airacobra – the XFL-1 Airabonita – had a tailwheel instead of a nose wheel, along with a tail hook for carrier landings, and under-wing radiators like a Spitfire. It got no further than a single prototype, which was found in deplorable condition in the 1970s on the shore of the Patuxent River, south of Washington, DC, where it had suffered the effects of many years of salt water splashing onto its aluminum skin.

Despite the lack of enthusiasm on the part of American and British air arms, Bell was determined to continue with plans for a next generation fighter, which turned out to be the P-63 Kingcobra.

Specifications of the P-39Q

Length: 30ft 2in
Wingspan: 34ft 0in
Height: 11ft 10in
Wing area: 213 sq ft
Maximum speed: 375mph at 15,000ft
Maximum range: 1,075 miles at 175mph with 175 gallon drop tank
Service ceiling: 35,000ft
Rate of climb: 2,500ft/min

Surviving Examples

P-39D
USAAF 41-6951 – Beck Military Collection

P-39F
one in a private collection

P-39K
Fantasy of Flight

P-39N
USAAF 42-19027 – Planes of Fame
USAAF 42-8740 – Yanks Air Museum
3 others

P-39Q
USAAF 42-20000 – March AFB
USAAF 44-2664 – Central Aviation Museum of Finland (ex-Red Air Force)

USAAF 42-20007 – Virginia Air & Space Center
USAAF 44-2433 – US National Air & Space Museum
USAAF 42-19993 – Imperial War Museum (Duxford)
USAAF 44-3908 – Kalamazoo Air Zoo
USAAF 44-2433 – National Museum of the USAF

P-400 (Bell designation for Airacobra I) two in private collections

Curtiss P-40 Tomahawk/Kittyhawk/Warhawk

The Curtiss P-40 was America's glamour airplane for the first part of the war, thanks in considerable part to the ferocious tiger-shark mouth painted on the nose of those flown by the China-based Flying Tigers. Like the eye-catching snowy owl decoration on the early 1930s Curtiss P-6 Hawks, it concealed marginal performance.

When the United States entered the war, the USAAF's P-40 was its best production fighter, with considerably better performance than the Navy's Grumman F4F Wildcat. Both, however, were inferior to the Japanese Zero in a dogfight, but could withstand far greater battle damage, and remained in combat until better airplanes became available.

The XP-40 was not merely a design development of the P-36, it was actually an early production P-36A with an Allison V-1710 V-12 engine supplanting its radial. Tests were so encouraging that an initial order for 524 airplanes was signed in April 1939, more than 18 months before America entered the war. Five months later, almost 200 had been delivered as P-40B Tomahawks. The remainder of those on order became Hawk 81 export models, originally promised to France, but diverted to the RAF as Tomahawk Is when France fell to the Germans.

First to fly the P-40 in combat were volunteer civilian pilots of a quasi-official unit composed of American pilots commanded by General Claire Chennault and known as the 'Flying Tigers'. Their successes over the Japanese constituted one of the few positive notes in the first few months after the attack on Pearl Harbor. After several months as the American Volunteer Group, they were absorbed into the USAAF and continued to plague the Japanese, who had previously faced little serious opposition.

Of the 900+ Tomahawks ordered for the RAF, many went to China and others to the USSR. The RAF used some of them for ground support in the Middle East from October 1941, while only a few of almost 100 based at Pearl Harbor in December 1941 survived the Japanese attack. Despite the emergence of much

superior American fighters, including the P-51 Mustang and F6F Hellcat, production of slightly improved P-40s was increased.

While early models of the P-40 were being produced, Curtiss began testing a follow-on airplane, the XP-46. As it offered no particular improvements over the latest P-40s, the program was cancelled. A second successor was in the works at the same time: the P-53, which was to have had a laminar-flow wing (like the P-51) and a 1,600hp Continental inverted V-12 engine. This became the XP-60, which, in turn, was tested with a variety of engines and propellers, resulting in a protracted test program. Before a reliable, high-performance airplane could be developed, all of the P-60 versions had become obsolete, and the long line that had begun with the XP-40 ended.

Surprisingly, the total production reached 13,738, even though its performance was never up to that of the Axis fighters it faced. Only the P-47 and P-51 were built in greater numbers. When the war ended, orders for 780 more of these long-obsolete fighters were cancelled.

Specifications of the P-40F

Length: 33ft 4in
Wingspan: 37ft 4in
Height: 10ft 7in
Wing area: 236 sq ft
Maximum speed: 364mph at 20,000ft
Maximum range: 1,500 miles with 175-gallon drop tank
Service ceiling: 34,400ft

Surviving Examples

P-40B
c/n 2380 – Imperial War Museum (Duxford)
National Air Museum of the US Navy

P-40C
Royal Thai Air Force Museum
USAAC 41-13390 – Flying Heritage Collection
Armed Forces Central Museum (Moscow)

P-40E
RCAF 1076 – Canadian National Air Museum,
USAAC 41-35927 – The Fighter Factory
USAAF 42-65406 – National Museum of the US Air Force
Fantasy of Flight

P-40F
One under restoration in Australia

P-40M
USAAF 42-105270 – Hill AFB
Two flying

TP-40M
USAAF 43-5802 – North Weald

P-40N
USAAF 42-105192 – Planes of Fame
USAAF 43-5788 – Kalamazoo (Michigan) Air Zoo
RAF FX760 – RAF Museum (Hendon)

TP-40N
USAAF 44-7084 – Palm Springs Air Museum
USAAF 44-47923 – Fantasy of Flight

Republic P-47 Thunderbolt
The long road marked by steady increases in power and improvements in streamlining began with the little Seversky P-35 and ended with the fastest propeller-driven fighters ever built. Along the way came the Republic P-47 Thunderbolt, built in greater numbers than any other American fighter. Despite its being the largest piston-powered, single-engined fighter ever to see combat in large numbers, it could hold its own against most enemy aircraft (a P-47 pilot was the first American to shoot down a German Me 262 jet), and proved to be one of the most effective fighter-bombers of the war.

The original XP-47A was to have been an Allison V-12-powered lightweight fighter, but was cancelled early in the program. The designation was reused for the next stage in the evolution of Alexander P de Seversky's fighters. The P-47B applied European combat experience to the Seversky designs and resulted in the Republic Aircraft Company's first important production project.

It differed from its predecessors in having greater armor protection for its pilot, along with better self-sealing fuel tanks. And more and larger machine guns. This demanded a major increase in power, which was supplied by the relatively new 18-cylinder, two-row Pratt & Whitney R-2800 Double Wasp engine, already rated at 2,000hp and destined for greatness.

The first version to enter large-scale production was the P-47C, which differed from the 'B' in many ways, most significant of which was a 200-gallon drop tank enabling it to escort bombers all the way into Germany. It got into combat in April 1943, at about the time the P-47D was first produced as its replacement. It was the 'D', of which more than 12,000 were built, that established the Thunderbolt as a major fighter in both the European and Pacific theaters of war, thanks in no small part to its eight .50 cal. machine guns in the wings.

The early D-models had the same cockpit canopy that faired into the turtledeck of earlier versions, but reports back from combat units resulted in most aircraft being refitted with a full bubble canopy providing much better rearward visibility. It was this version that gained a reputation for durability and versatility

Even before production versions of the Thunderbolt had reached the 425mph mark, prototypes were being tested that were aimed at much higher speeds. The XP-47H, with an experimental 2,300hp Chrysler V-16, hit 490mph in level flight, but the engine never

went into production. The XP-47J used a standard R-2800, but was a lighter version with a very tight cowl and other improvements that enabled it to be the only piston-engined fighter ever to exceed 500mph, when it was clocked at 504mph in 1944.

While the P-47J was not built in quantity, its ideas justified the design of the Republic P-72 with an even cleaner cowl, thanks to the under-fuselage mounting of most of the air intake for a huge 3,500hp P&W R-4360 Wasp Major. Top speed with full military equipment was 490mph but, like so many new and highly promising airplanes, it was dropped in favor of jets, with their far greater potential for development. Total production of all models of the P-47 was 15,677. Orders for an additional 5,934 were cancelled when the war ended.

Specifications of the P-47

Length: 36ft 2in
Wingspan: 40ft 9in
Height: 14ft 7in
Wing area: 300 sq ft
Maximum speed: 426mph at 30,000ft
Maximum range: 1,800 miles at 231mph at 10,000ft with drop tanks
Service ceiling: 42,000ft
Rate of climb: 3,120ft/min

Surviving Examples

P-47B
three under restoration

P-47D
(turtledeck USAAF 42-23278 and bubble-canopied 45-49167) – National Museum of the USAF
USAAF 44-32691 – US National Air & Space Museum
USAAF 45-49181 – Kalamazoo Air Zoo
USAAF 45-49458 – New England Air Museum
USAAF 44-20371 – Musee de l'Air
USAAF 42-8130 – Pima Air and Space Museum
USAAF 44-89746 – Italian Air Force Museum
USAAF 45-49295 – RAF Museum (Cosford)
USAAF 45-49406 – Flying Heritage Collection

P-47G
USAAF 42-25068 – The Fighter Collection
USAAF 42-25234 – Planes of Fame

P-47N
USAAF 44-89320 – Eglin AFB
USAAF 44-89348 – Lackland AFB
USAAF 45-89448 – Cradle of Aviation Museum

North American P-51 Mustang

The P-51 is widely regarded as the finest all-around fighter plane of World War Two. Prior to the first flight of the prototype XP-51 in October 1940, North American Aviation had built a grand total of 13 pursuit planes. What became the Mustang resulted from a request from the British for a second factory to build Curtiss Hawk 87As (P-40s), which NAA rejected, preferring to design a completely new airplane. The deadline for completion of the prototype of what became the Mustang was just four months away, which would be unthinkable today, but was actually beaten by several days.

Two airplanes were pulled from the first batch of the British order and became the US Army Air Corps' XP-51 prototypes, one of which made the type's first flight on 26 October 1940. Six months later, the first production P-51 flew. Thanks to its radical laminar-flow wing and exceptionally clean basic design, it immediately out-performed everything else in American skies. Its 1,200hp Allison V-1710 engine drove it to almost 400mph, and its armament of four 20mm cannon was a first for an American fighter.

The only drawback to the new airplane was its engine, which lacked performance at high altitude.

The first British airplanes went into combat in July 1942 with four .30 cal. and four .50 cal. machine guns. Known as the Mustang I, they were used for tactical reconnaissance and ground support. Hundreds more were ordered for the RAF and USAAF, all of them powered by Allisons, and many designated as A-36A Apache dive bombers.

Two P-51As became XP-51Bs when retrofitted with 1,400hp, supercharged Rolls-Royce Merlin V-12s, built by the Packard Motor Car Company. Top speed at altitude immediately jumped to 440mph, considerably faster than any other Allied or Axis fighter. The Mustang's reputation was made, with subsequent six-gun P-51Bs and P-51Cs (depending on which factory built them) using what was by then called the V-1650 engine.

The final major change was to a bubble canopy, which cost a few mph, but permitted much improved visibility in combat. Thus equipped, the P-51D became the major production version, with almost 8,000 being built. Normal range of just under 1,000 miles was doubled with a pair of teardrop-shaped, 110-US gallon drop tanks under the wings, which allowed Mustangs to escort heavy

bombers all the way from England to Berlin and back. Almost 500 were converted into unarmed F-6 photoplanes.

With the development of the D-model at its limit, a major redesign of the entire airplane was undertaken, resulting in the P-51H, whose maximum speed of 487mph at 25,000ft was the greatest of any propeller-driven production fighter of the war. It had a new, thinner wing lacking the 'broken' leading edge, thanks to its smaller main wheels and disc brakes. The vertical tail had greater height and area to help balance the increased power of its Packard Merlin V-1650-9 engine, ultimately rated at a maximum of 2,220hp. Five hundred and fifty were built during the war, and many were used in the final stages of the Pacific War. Cancelled at V-J Day were 1,445 P-51Hs and 1,700 P-51Ls, this latter which was to have the even more powerful V-1650-11 engine.

The German answer to the increasingly superior Mustangs, which they had to face with fewer and slower airplanes flown by poorly-trained pilots, was the entry into combat of insufficiently tested jet- and rocket-powered fighters. Their far greater speed was not enough to regain air superiority, and Allied pilots developed new tactics to deal with the initially intimidating new airplanes.

Whether protecting bombers or dogfighting with Messerschmitts, Focke Wulfs or Zeros, or taking aerial photos from great altitude, the Mustang proved superior in all theaters of war. Total production was 14,066 airplanes, not counting the 4,723 more that were cancelled when the war ended. Of the total built, almost 8,000 were P-51Ds.

Specifications for the P-51D

Length: 32ft 3in
Wingspan: 37ft 0in
Height: 8ft 8in
Wing area: 233 sq ft
Maximum speed: 437mph at 25,000ft
Maximum range: 2,080 miles at 244mph at 10,000ft, with two 110-gallon drop tanks
Service ceiling: 41,900ft
Rate of climb: 2,940ft/min

Surviving Examples

XP-51
USAAC 41-38 – Experimental Aircraft Association Museum

P-51A
USAAF 43-6251 – Planes of Fame
USAAF 43-6274 – Yanks Air Museum

P-51B
USAAF 43-12252 – auto racing entrepreneur Jack Roush

P-51C
USAAF 44-10947 – US National Air & Space Museum
USAAF '42-106449' – The Fighter Collection
USAAF 42-103831 – Fantasy of Flight

P-51D
USAAF 44-72364 – Flying Heritage Collection – almost every American air museum, many others around the world, 100+ flying, 230 in private and public collections

TP-51D
USAAF 44-84847 – The Fighter Collection

XP-51G
USAAF 43-43335 or 43-43336 – under restoration in La Canada, California

P-51H
USAAF 44-64376 – Lackland AFB
USAAF 44-64625 – Chanute Aerospace Museum, at least two flying

P-51K
USAAF 44-11811 – Israeli Air Force Museum
USAAF 44-12125 – Soesterburg Air Base, Netherlands
USAAF 44-12840 – actor Tom Cruise
USAAF 44-12216 – Crawford Aviation & Auto Museum (#80 racer)

TP-51
Planes of Fame

Mk.IV
RCAF 9298 – Canadian National Air Museum

Commonwealth Aircraft Co.
CA-17
RAAF A68-39 – Tillamook Air Museum

CA-18
RAAF A68-137 – RAAF Museum
RAAF A58-187 – Astronaut Frank Borman

A-36A
USAAF 42-83665 – National Museum of the US Air Force
USAAF 42-83738 – Warhawk Air Museum

Curtiss P-55 Ascender

In November 1939, a full two years before America entered the war, the US Army Air Corps announced its interest in pursuit designs of 'an unconventional nature'. They were to be powered by the very new Pratt & Whitney R-2600 engine, rated at approximately 2,000hp from its 24-cylinder 'H' design, and lighter and smaller than current engines. Designs for this competition included the Vultee XP-54 twin-boom pusher, the Northrop XP-56 Black Bullet semi-flying-wing, and the tail-first Curtiss XP-55 Ascender.

Other countries – including Italy and Japan – tested tail-first fighter designs, but none was ever placed in production.

The goal of the Air Corps competition was not so much to build different-looking airplanes, but to take advantage of the opportunities for better streamlining and improved pilot visibility offered by novel arrangements of wings and tails. The problems posed by radical shapes included control in normal flight and during spins.

A steady stream of problems convinced Pratt & Whitney that it was not worth the effort to proceed with such a radical engine design, so it was cancelled. The XP-55 thus received a V-1710 Allison V-12, rated at 500hp less than the original Pratt & Whitney, which guaranteed a drop in performance.

Prior to building the first of three prototypes ordered by the USAAC, Curtiss built a full-scale test vehicle with a 275hp Menasco straight-six, air-cooled engine. Test flights, numbering almost 170, demonstrated that major additions to the vertical tail area eased but did not completely cure the directional stability problem. Initially the airplane was to have been armed with two 20mm cannon and two .50 cal. machine guns. This was soon changed to four machine guns, fewer than any contemporary production fighter.

The first XP-55 prototype was flown in July 1943, but was lost the following November when its test pilot was unable to recover from an inverted flat spin. The second and third airplanes were flown in January and April 1944. An extensive test program revealed more problems, this time with the lack of warning prior to a stall, and a great loss in altitude during recovery from the ensuing spin. Added to this was insufficient engine cooling at certain flight attitudes.

The final blow resulted from tests which showed the top speed to be well below that of fighters that were already in squadron service. There was also concern over the system that was to have enabled the pilot to jettison the propeller immediately prior to baling out in an emergency. The prospect, however slim, of hitting the prop would hardly have endeared the airplane to those who were to have flown it in combat. The P-55 was clearly obsolete before it ever could have entered production. Neither Curtiss nor any other American manufacturer is known to have considered this style of airplane for any future projects.

Specifications for the XP-55

Length: 29ft 7in
Wingspan: 44ft 1in
Height: 10ft 1in
Wing area: 235 sq ft
Empty weight: 6,350lb
Maximum speed: 378mph at 16,900ft
Maximum range: 1,440 miles
Service ceiling: 34,600ft
Rate of climb: 7:06 to 20,000ft

Surviving Example

XP-55
USAAF 42-78846 – US National Air & Space Museum

Northrop P-56 Black Bullet

The biggest loser in the three-design competition for a radical fighter was the most radical, being a semi-flying wing with a rear-mounted engine driving contra-rotating propellers. Developed by Northrop, which had more experience with flying wings than any other company in the world, it was the smallest of the three. Having as much power, it certainly should have been faster, with an estimated top speed of 465mph at high altitude.

The wing design had already been shown to be eminently flyable during tests on the little N-1M, a true flying wing, powered by a pair of 65hp Lycoming light plane engines. That test-bed had no vertical tail surfaces at all, and was the first such John K Northrop design to fly.

When the 2,000hp Pratt & Whitney H-style engine was dropped by the manufacturer due to excessive development problems, it

was replaced by a proven 2,000hp P&W R-2800 Double Wasp. Northrop engineers were concerned about installing a much larger and heavier engine in their carefully designed airplane, but there was no convenient alternative on the horizon.

The first XP-56 began taxi tests in April 1943, but ground handling and engine installation problems delayed the first flight until September. Several very low-altitude flights were made until a tire blew out during taxying and the airplane was wrecked. Major changes to the weight and balance and to the vertical tail surfaces were made to the second and third prototypes. In addition, an unusual type of aileron control was built, having split flaps which opened to produce drag on one side.

The second airplane didn't fly until March 1944, and then revealed a disturbing tendency to hug the ground until quite high runway speeds were attained. By this time, it had become apparent in wind tunnel tests that the XP-56 would not achieve its promised maximum speed. Other problems, including much higher than anticipated fuel consumption, were making it obvious that turning test airplanes into production airplanes would involve far greater time and effort than was considered reasonable.

The XP-56 was retired, leaving none of the fascinating radical designs as much more than interesting but unsuccessful engineering exercises. Not one of them led directly to any future airplane designs.

Specifications of the XP-56

Length: 27ft 6in
Wingspan: 42ft 6in
Height:
Wing area: 306 sq ft

Empty weight: 8,700lb
Estimated Maximum speed: 465mph at 25,000ft
Estimated range: 660 miles
Estimated Rate of climb: 3,125ft/min
Estimated Service ceiling: 33,000ft

Surviving Example

XP-56
USAAF 42-38353 – US National Air & Space Museum

Bell P-59 Airacomet

The United States entered the jet age late. Nazi Germany had flown the Heinkel He 176 rocket-powered airplane in June 1939, and the Heinkel He 178 turbojet in August 1939. The Italians flew a pseudo-turbojet – the Caproni Campini CC.2 – in August 1940, with an engine whose compressor was powered by a piston engine. The

British flew their pioneering turbojet-powered Gloster E.28/39 in May 1941.

It wasn't until October 1942, that the first American jet-propelled airplane – the Bell XP-59 – was flown at Muroc Army Air Field, later to become Edwards AFB, north of Los Angeles.

The contract for the P-59 was awarded to Bell Aircraft Company, despite its spotty record, because it wasn't as busy as the other major airframe manufacturers. Additionally, it was close to the General Electric Company, whose experience with turbo-superchargers had put it in a good position to begin development of jet engines based on the Whittle engine, one of the first of which was given to the US as part of the very effective Anglo–American technical exchange program.

While the XP-59 designation had already been used for a Bell twin-boom pusher fighter design that had been cancelled, it was reused in hopes of keeping the existence of the radical new type of military airplane secret for as long as possible.

Powered by a pair of GE 1-A engines rated at 1,400lb of thrust (1lb = 1hp at 350mph), the first XP-59A was trucked to Muroc Dry Lake with a crude wooden propeller attached to its nose to fool any curious (and naïve) motorists encountered along the way. The first test flight was surprisingly uneventful, in view of all the novel ideas packed into the airplane, but subsequent tests showed that the top speed was barely 400mph.

Thirteen YP-59As for service tests used more powerful versions of the basic engine, but showed hardly any improvement in performance. It was just a large, gentle, slow-flying airplane, despite its very strange sound. Two of them became US Navy XF2L-1s and gave the sea-going service its first experience with jets.

The USAAF ordered 100 P-59As even before the XP-59 had flown, cutting the order in half when its poor performance became

known. Bell was starting design work on a much improved P-59B, but the project was transferred to Lockheed Aircraft Company where it became the P-80 Shooting Star. The remaining 66 Airacomets were demoted to trainers, where they performed well.

Bell went on to build an improved P-59, the larger, heavier XP-83, which might have become a long-range fighter, except that its overall performance was not up to standard. It was the company's final attempt to build a fighter.

Specifications of the P-59A

Length: 38ft 10in
Wingspan: 45ft 6in
Height: 12ft 4in
Wing area: 356 sq ft
Empty weight: 7,950lb
Maximum speed: 413mph at 30,000ft
Maximum range: 520 miles at 290mph at 20,000ft with two 150-gallon drop tanks
Service ceiling: 46,200ft

Surviving Examples

XP-59
USAAF 42-108784 – US National Air & Space Museum

YP-59A
USAAF 44-108777 – Planes of Fame

P-59A
USAAF 44-22609 – National Museum of the US Air Force

Northrop P-61 Black Widow

The Black Widow has the unusual distinction of being forced off the USAAF's secret list when accurate sketches of it appeared in a widely read newspaper comic strip. Its author/artist lived near Eglin AAF, Florida, saw it repeatedly flying over his home as it was being tested and assumed it was known to the public.

On 21 May 1942, the prototype XP-61 became the first purpose-built night fighter to fly. And while a few developmental Heinkel He 219s were rushed into service in 1943, the production version didn't get into action until August 1944, two months after the Black Widow became the first production night fighter to see action.

Until the P-61 came on the scene, night fighters had been day fighters or light bombers equipped with the rapidly developing radar with which enemy aircraft could be tracked with increasing precision in the pitch dark. But these airplanes were being used in a manner not foreseen by their designers, and steady increases in weight due to more and more electronics and weapons reduced their performance.

To solve the problem, Northrop proposed a twin-engined fighter the size of a B-25 Mitchell medium bomber. It was to have a three-man crew: pilot, radar operator and gunner, the latter responsible for operating as many as four 20mm cannon in a top turret and four fixed .50 cal. machine guns mounted in a streamlined bulge under the fuselage.

For power, it used a pair of 18-cylinder Pratt & Whitney R-2800 two-row radial engines that initially developed 2,000hp and eventually as much as 2,800hp. With external fuel tanks, a P-61A had a cruising range of almost 2,000 miles, especially valuable in the south Pacific, where the nearest friendly landing field could be hundreds of miles of ocean away. More than 3,000lb of bombs could be slung from wing shackles. It was completely unlike any fighter when the first P-61As began to replace Douglas A-20 attack bombers that had been hurriedly converted into P-70 night fighters.

To answer the need for a version that would fly faster and higher, Northrop produced the P-61C with engines now turbo-supercharged and uprated to 2,800hp, giving a top speed of 430mph at 30,000 feet, and a service ceiling of 41,000 feet.

The total production of 691 included 80 P-61, 120 P-61A, 450 P-61B and 41 P-61C, with another 475 being cancelled at war's end.

After the war, the USAAF operated stripped-down P-61s in the form of F-15 photo planes. A dozen P-61As were transferred to the US Marine Corps immediately after the war, as F2T-1s. By then the Northrop Corporation had returned to flying wings, starting with the XP-56 Black Bullet, then the XP-79 prone-pilot jet fighter and finally the huge B-35 and YB-49 flying wing bombers.

Specifications for the P-61B

Length: 48ft 11in
Wingspan: 66ft 0in
Height: 14ft 2in
Wing area: 664 sq ft
Empty weight: 20,965lb
Maximum speed: 369mph at 20,000ft
Maximum range: 1,900 miles at 221mph at 10,000ft with external fuel
Service ceiling: 33,100ft
Rate of climb: 2,270ft/min

Surviving Examples

P-61B
USAAF 42-39445 – being restored at the Mid-Atlantic Air Museum

P-61C
USAAF 43-8330 – US National Air & Space Museum
USAAF 43-8353 – National Museum of the US Air Force
Beijing Aeronautic Institute

Bell P-63 Kingcobra

With its P-39 Airacobra obviously not the world-beater that the manufacturer had hoped and claimed, a major redesign was put into motion in early 1941, resulting in the P-63 Kingcobra. Like its predecessor, its mid-mounted Allison V-1710 engine lacked high-altitude performance. Unlike the P-39, it never served in a combat role with the USAAF, with most of the 3,500 produced going to the Soviet Air Force which welcomed its low-altitude speed, heavy firepower and ability to absorb punishment.

While the P-63 was considered a completely new airplane, it strongly resembled a slightly enlarged P-39 with about 200 additional horsepower from its newer Allison V-12 engine.

The first contract was signed in June 1941, for two prototypes based on tests with modified P-39s. The first XP-63 flew on 7 December 1942, and deliveries of the first production P-63As began less than a year later. Within a year, more than 1,700 had been built, with most going to the USSR for ground-support use, along with 300 sent to France.

The only American operation of Kingcobras was with 100 RP-63A, 200 RP-63C and 32 RP-63G in a novel air-to-air gunnery

training program. With fuselage sides heavily armored, student pilots fired at them with frangible bullets which shattered on impact, each strike being signaled by a red light on the target airplane and a counter inside.

A total of 3,303 P-63s was built, and another 3,350 were cancelled at V-J Day. Bell's subsequent efforts to create fighter planes were limited to the little XP-77, an experiment in lightweight design that other nations were trying and failing at. While the two prototypes weighed a mere 2,850lb empty, they came up far short of performance estimates and were quietly retired, thus ending a major era for the Bell Aircraft Company.

Specifications of the P-63A

Length: 32ft 8in
Wingspan: 38ft 4in
Height: 12ft 7in
Wing area: 248 sq ft
Empty weight: 6,375lb
Maximum speed: 410mph at 25,000ft.
Maximum range: 2,575 miles
Service ceiling: 43,000ft
Rate of climb: 7:18 to 25,000ft

Surviving Examples

P-63A
USAAF 42-68864 – Palm Springs Air Museum
USAAF 42-69080 – Yanks Air Museum
USAAF 42-69021 – ex-astronaut Frank Borman

RP-63A
USAAF 42-70255 – National Air & Space Museum

P-63C
USAAF 42-69775, 44-4011 – Russian Air Force Museum
Aircraft Restoration Co.
Yankee Air Corps

RP-63C
USAAF 44-4126 – Fantasy of Flight
USAAF 43-11223 – Frank Borman

P-63E
USAAF 43-11727 – National Museum of the USAF
USAAF 43-11727 – Pima Air and Space Museum
two restoration projects

P-63F
USAAF 43-11719 – Commemorative Air Force

RP-63G
USAAF 45-57295 – Lackland AFB

North American P-64
Starting in 1935, the new North American Aviation, Inc. struggled along by building small numbers of training and pursuit monoplanes based on its NA-16 basic trainer. The best-known result of this small-scale effort was the wartime AT-6/SNJ/Harvard series of advanced trainers which had no equal in the world.

Much less well known was the series of single- and two-seat trainers and ground-support airplanes which began with the NA-50A. The first NAA product with retractable landing gear, its success was limited to a sale of seven to the air force of Peru. Six examples of a pursuit variation – the NA-68 – were sold to the Royal Thai Air Force, and carried two .30 cal. machine guns and two 20mm cannon.

The six were on a ship bound for Thailand and briefly stopped in Hawaii when Thailand was invaded by the Japanese. The airplanes were immediately grabbed by the neutral United States, de-militarized and used as advanced trainers, even though they were still called *P-64*.

Only one has survived and has long been the property of the Experimental Aircraft Association, which flew it in displays for several years and then placed it on static display in its museum in Oshkosh, Wisconsin.

Specifications of the P-64

Length: 27ft 0in
Wingspan: 37ft 3in
Height: 9ft 8in
Wing area: 228 sq ft
Empty weight: 4,660lb
Maximum speed: 270mph at 8,700ft
Maximum range: 965 miles
Service ceiling: 27,500ft
Rate of climb:

Surviving Example

P-64
USAAC 41-19086 – Experimental Aircraft Association Museum

Fisher P-75 Eagle

The P-75 was designed and built by the Fisher Body Division of General Motors, then the world's largest producer of automobiles. In an effort to reduce design time, it combined proven parts from different successful airplanes. The wing used outer panels from a P-51 Mustang (in an inverted-gull arrangement like the F4U Corsair), the tail was from a Douglas SBD Dauntless carrier-based dive bomber, and the landing gear was from an F4U Corsair fighter.

All of these were arranged into a single airframe to be powered by the still-experimental Allison W-3420 engine. This ambitious engine was the result of coupling two V-12 Allison V-1710 engines, like those used in the P-38, P-39 and P-40. The resultant 3,420 cubic inch power plant had 24 cylinders in a 'W' arrangement. With the help of a complicated supercharging system, the W-3420 was rated at a maximum of 2,885hp at 3,000 rpm.

Several airplanes were fitted with one or more of these engines. The enormous Douglas B-19 had four of them, Lockheed's Black Widow-like XP-58 Chain Lightning had a pair, Boeing's souped-up B-29, called the XB-39, had four. None of these airplanes went into production, and so experience with the W-3420 in flight was severely limited, and in realistic operations, nil. In the XP-75, power was applied via one of the first contra-rotating propellers to be fitted to a fighter design.

The P-75 was aimed at a USAAF requirement for a fast-climbing interceptor, and had an estimated climb rate of 4,200 feet/minute. The first prototype flew on 17 November 1943, after the USAAF had decided it had a greater need for long-range escort fighters and had ordered six more XP-75 to be tested for that role. By then it had outer wing panels from a Curtiss P-40 and re-shaped tail surfaces to improve its stall-recovery.

Troubles followed upon troubles. The engines had cooling problems and failed to produce their advertised horsepower. The airplane suffered from instability and needed more effective ailerons. By the latter part of 1944, the first production model was about to enter its flight test stage when the USAAF decided it had all the well-proven long-range escort fighters it needed, and cancelled all but six of the production airplanes from an initial order of 2,500.

Preliminary tests showed the P-75A falling well short of the performance of the P-51 Mustang and P-47 Thunderbolt, and so

the entire project was ended with an understandable feeling of failure. It was a quaint airframe design idea, using an engine that had not been fully tested, and so it wasn't long before General Motors went back to what it knew best: building cars. The Eagle had no successor nor any obvious impact on future designs.

Specifications of the XP-75

Length: 40ft 5in
Wingspan: 49ft 4in
Height: 15ft 6in
Wing area: 347 sq ft
Empty weight: 11,495lb
Estimated Maximum speed: 433mph at 20,000ft

Estimated Maximum range: 3,500 miles at 314mph at 20,000ft with external fuel
Estimated Service ceiling: 36,400ft
Rate of climb: 4,200ft/min
Surviving Example

XP-75A

USAAF 44-44553 – US National Air & Space Museum (at the National Museum of the USAF)

Lockheed P-80 Shooting Star

Lockheed's XP-80 started out as the Bell XP-59B, which was to have been a much improved version of the lackluster Bell Airacomet. As Bell's production capacity was full with other projects, the new airplane was shifted to Lockheed. There, it was quickly redesigned by some of the top aeronautical engineers into America's first operational jet fighter.

In less than five months, it was flown as the P-80 Shooting Star on 9 January 1944, topping 500mph on its first flight. The XP-80 production prototype was powered by a British-built de Havilland Goblin turbojet rated at 2,400lb of thrust. It demonstrated excellent flying qualities, soon besting the USAAF's top fighters in mock combat. With those engines unavailable for further use, the XP-80A production prototypes had a highly modified version – the GE J-33 engine rated at 3,850lb.

So successful was the design that the USAAF ordered 5,000, many of which were to be built by North American Aviation. Top speed soon exceeded that of the fastest American propeller-driven fighter – the North American P-51H – by almost 100mph. It was also superior in its rate of climb and service ceiling, while its range was almost as great.

Only 917 P-80A's were produced, those remaining being cancelled at V-J Day, though almost 800 F-80B's and F-80C's with uprated engines were built after the war.

Perhaps the type's greatest impact was as a trainer. By stretching the fuselage and adding a back seat, it became the USAF T-33 and US Navy TV-2, with more than 4,000 built. They remained in the service of many countries for many years, as the first popular jet trainer. With guns and radar, it then became the F-94 Starfire interceptor.

One more version of the P-80 made its mark in the history books. The XP-80R, with its boosted engine, enlarged air intakes and lowered canopy, was used by Colonel Al Boyd to set a World Speed Record of 623.73mph at Muroc Air Base (now Edwards AFB), north of Los Angeles, on 19 June 1947. It had been almost 12 years since the absolute record had been held by an American pilot.

No Shooting Star or any other type of American jet fighter was used in combat during World War Two, though two were sent to Europe to acquaint USAAF pilots and ground crews with the new techniques needed to operate this radical new type of fighter.

Specifications of the P-80A

Length: 34ft 6in
Wingspan: 38ft 11in
Height: 11ft 4in
Wing area: 238 sq ft
Empty weight: 7,920lb
Maximum speed: 558mph at sea level
Maximum range: 1,320 miles at 407mph at 25,000ft with two 165-gallon drop tanks
Service ceiling: 45,000ft
Rate of climb: 4,150ft/min

Surviving Examples

XP-80
USAAF 44-83020 – National Air & Space Museum

P-80A
USAAF 44-85182 – Kalamazoo Air Zoo
USAAF 44-85488 – Planes Of Fame

P-80B
USAAF 45-8612 – Pima Air and Space Museum

P-80C
USAAF 45-8490 – Castle AFB Air Museum
USAF 48-0868 – EAA Museum,
USAF 49-0853 – National Museum of the USAF (at Holloman, New Mexico AFB)

P-80R
USAAF 44-85200 – National Museum of the US Air Force

Vultee P-81

While the new jet-propelled fighters were unquestionably the fastest things in the sky as World War Two came to an end, they were far from fully developed. They lacked rapid acceleration and long range when compared to the latest piston-engined fighters. In an effort to solve these problems, the Consolidated Vultee Aircraft Corporation proposed a fighter with both a jet engine and one of the even newer turbo-prop engines. It was to be armed with no fewer than six .50 cal. machine guns and six 20mm cannon.

Neither Consolidated nor its Vultee subsidiary had much recent experience in building fighters, and Consolidated's last production pursuit for the US Army was a series of 54 P-30s in the mid-1930s. Since then it had specialized in heavy bombers, producing 18,000 B-24 Liberators. Vultee, which had built the unsuccessful P-54 twin-boom fighter and then manufactured almost 150 P-66

Vanguard pursuits for Sweden, had gone into mass production, turning out 9,500 BT-13 and BT-15 Valiant basic trainers.

The original plan had been to install a 2,300hp GE TG-100 turboprop engine in the nose and a 3,750lb Allison J-33 turbojet in the tail. The former would be for acceleration and long-range cruising, while the latter would be for top speed. The turboprop was not ready when the airframe needed it, in January 1945, and was temporarily replaced with a 1,600hp Packard-built Rolls-Royce Merlin. The turboprop, while of the correct type, turned out to develop a mere 1,400hp, and so the airplane had little more than half its design power. By the time the turboprop was improved and installed, its power remained little more than that of the piston engine.

The performance on reduced power turned out to be irrelevant, as the Pacific war had progressed close enough to Japan such that there was no longer any need for this unusually long-ranged escort fighter.

No official performance tests were performed by the US Army, and so all that is available comes from the manufacturer and must be considered estimates with the full-power originally planned, with appropriate reductions figured in to compensate for natural bragging.

Specifications of the XP-81

Length: 44ft 10in
Wingspan: 50ft 6in
Height: 14ft 0in
Wing area: 425 sq ft
Empty weight: 12,755lb
Maximum speed: 507mph at 30,000ft

Maximum range: 2,500 miles at 275mph at 25,000
Service ceiling: 35,500ft
Rate of climb: 5,300ft/min

Surviving Example

XP-81
USAAF 44-91000 (with parts from 44-91001) – Edwards AFB Museum

North American P-82 Twin Mustang

Of all the unusual fighter designs proposed to the US Army Air Forces during the war, the only one that proved truly successful was the twin-fuselage P-82 Twin Mustang. Like several other designs, it was intended as a long-range escort fighter in the Pacific, where the distances between remote island airfields required long over-water flights. An additional concern was the fatigue being experienced by solo pilots on such long fighter missions.

25 5in air-to-ground rockets. Clearly, the airplane was meant for more than escorting bombers.

The end of the war a few months later resulted in all but 20 of the 500 airplanes being cancelled. After the war, several more versions were developed, including night fighters. These and 100 F-82Es that were very much like the P-82B, served during the Korean War.

The Twin Mustang turned out to be the last piston-engined fighter to be built for the USAAF. The example in the National Museum of the USAF is 'Betty-Jo', which in 1947 was flown 5,051 miles from Hawaii to New York, the longest non-stop, non-refueled flight by a piston-engined fighter.

North American built no more propeller-driven fighters, but went on to produce great numbers of F-86 Sabre and F-100 Super Sabre jet fighters.

To solve the latter problem, the manufacturer joined two P-51H-like fuselages to a new center section and two standard outer wing panels. One cockpit would have a full set of controls and instruments, while the other would have controls and limited instrumentation and would be used by the relief pilot. Possible problems that could be experienced when flying from an off-set position were first tested on a P-38 that had an extra cockpit out on one boom.

During the design stage, the fuselages were extended by almost four feet, the main landing gear, previously mounted under the wings, was moved to the fuselages, and opposite-rotation late-model Rolls-Royce Merlin engines were installed. Regardless of the changes, the resulting airplane looked very much like two standard Mustangs flying in very close formation.

The first flight of the XP-82 was made on 15 April 1945. The USAAF ordered 500 similar P-82Bs with six .50 cal. machine guns in the center section, and wing racks for 4,000lb of bombs or

Specifications of the P-82B

Length: 38ft 1in
Wingspan: 51ft 3in
Height: 8ft 2in
Wing area: 408 sq ft
Empty weight: 13,405lb
Maximum speed: 482mph at 25,100ft
Maximum range: 1,390 miles at 227mph with normal fuel load
Service ceiling: 41,600ft

Surviving Examples

P-82B
USAAF 44-65162 – Museum of Flight (Santa Monica)
USAAF 44-65168 – National Museum of the US Air Force

Chapter Two
US Navy

Brewster F2A-1 (B-239) Buffalo

The Buffalo was Brewster Aeronautical Co.'s first production airplane. It was the US Navy's first all-metal, carrier-based monoplane. It also may have been the Navy's least successful combat airplane.

It started out as the winner of a Navy competition for a pursuit to replace the Grumman F3F biplane, besting the XFN-1 (navalized Seversky P-35) and the XF4F-1, an improved Grumman F3F. Initially it had outstanding maneuverability and was the only one of the three able to exceed 300mph. On the negative side, it lacked the armor, speed and range to stand up to more modern fighters then entering combat.

To solve its problems, Brewster added armor plating and fuel, the result being an increase in weight that degraded its maneuverability and once-good handling characteristics. As other Allied and Axis fighters improved, the Buffalo was doing the opposite. Moreover, production slowed, which was eventually blamed on mismanagement on the part of the still-young manufacturer.

Other air forces, desperately in need of fighters, ordered the original F2A-1, with Finland, Great Britain, Belgium and the Netherlands East Indies placing sizeable orders. Some were redirected when the country which had placed the order was knocked out of the war. The British, in particular, rejected the F2A-2 Buffalo when its more powerful engine revealed serious maintenance problems. Even the US Navy ran into difficulties with the airplane, whose landing gear was unable to survive the high stresses of carrier landings.

When the Buffalo entered combat against the Japanese, the Zero's far superior maneuverability and rate of climb made the Brewster airplane an easy target, and most were shot down soon after entering combat.

Only Finland had a happy experience with the tubby little fighter. After being modified to meet local requirements, 43 Buffaloes, piloted by dedicated and well-trained Finns, fought the Soviet Air Force in 1941–1944, and the Luftwaffe in 1944 and 1945, achieving a level of success unknown to the other air forces operating them. According to Finnish aviation historian Eino Rittaranta, almost 500 enemy (mainly Soviet) airplanes were shot down by Buffalo pilots, one of whom is credited with 41 victories.

An attempt to produce the Buffalo in Finland led to the Humu, a very similar fighter built primarily of non-strategic wood and, being considerably heavier than the original metal design, with even poorer performance. The sole prototype has been restored and placed on public view.

Specifications of the F2A-1

Length: 26ft 4in
Wingspan: 35ft 0in
Height: 12ft 1in
Wing area: 209 sq ft
Empty weight: 4,730lb
Maximum speed: 313mph at 13,500ft
Maximum range: 840 miles
Service ceiling: 30,675ft
Rate of climb: 2,070ft/min

Surviving Example

F2A-1
Finnish AF BW372 –Aviation Museum of Central Finland

Curtiss F15C

There was hardly a year that Curtiss wasn't building at least one type of airplane for the US military. From 1911, when Curtiss delivered a Model D for the US Army Signal Corps, through 1945 when it built a trio of prototype XF15C-1 fighters for the US Navy, it was a major supplier of fighters, dive bombers, scouts, transports and trainers.

But by the mid-point of the war it was apparent that the ability of the old-line manufacturer to create first-line airplanes was fading. Its last serious effort for the Navy was a large twin-engined fighter intended to operate from carriers. With a combination of piston and jet power, it was meant to fly faster, climb faster and range farther than any previous propeller-driven Navy fighter. Like so many other promising designs of that era, it found itself competing with airplanes powered by pure turbojet engines that had much brighter futures.

Unlike previous carrier fighters, it had tricycle landing gear and a bubble canopy. But it also weighed more than 12,000lb empty, rising to a fully-loaded 18,700lb. That would pose quite a challenge even for its 2,000hp Pratt & Whitney R-2800 radial engine and de Havilland Goblin jet engine, built by Allis-Chalmers and rated at 2,700lb of thrust.

The first XF15C-1 flew on just its piston engine on 27 February 1945 but was destroyed in a crash barely three months later. The second prototype flew in July and the third a short time later, both having a T-tail. Testing began at the Navy's Patuxent River Flight Test Center, but was soon stopped so that efforts could be concentrated on the likes of McDonnell's jet-engined FH-1 Phantom.

With that, Curtiss-Wright ended its decades of airplane manufacturing for the US Navy. The government-owned Columbus,

Ohio, factory where the XF15C-1s (as well as SB2C Helldivers and lesser types) had been built was turned over to North American Aviation, Inc., still relatively new in the business of military airplanes, but with a much better future.

Specifications

Length: 44ft
Wingspan: 48ft
Height: 15ft 3in
Wing area: 400 sq ft
Empty weight: 12,650lb

Maximum speed: 470mph at 23,500ft
Maximum range: 1,385 miles
Service ceiling: 41,800 ft
Rate of climb: 5,000ft/min

Surviving Example

XF15C-1
BuAer 01214 – Quonset Air Museum

Grumman F4F Wildcat

It was time for the US Navy to modernize its fleet of pursuit planes. The strut-braced biplane had seen its days of romance and glory and the cantilever (internally-braced) monoplane was starting to appear in many portions of the sky. There remained concerns over the strength of cantilever wings and over the higher landing speeds of more streamlined airplanes. But with the rapid growth in power of aircraft engines, and advances in structural engineering, the change was inevitable. Especially since potential enemies were clearly headed in that direction.

For the Navy, tradition was a major obstacle. The men who made the decisions had known only biplanes during their flying careers, and were hesitant to change what to them seemed to be working well.

But speed was all-important in aerial combat, and there was no question that all those struts and wires were holding the Navy back. The first monoplane to be ordered into development was the Brewster F2A Buffalo, in 1936. At the same time the latest in Grumman's line of rotund biplanes – the F4F-1 – was approved, just in case the new style didn't pan out.

Grumman's FF-1, F2F and F3F had been mainstays of the carrier force since 1931, thanks to their rugged construction and (rare for that era) retractable landing gear. It quickly became apparent that the new Grumman biplane would offer little improvement over its immediate predecessor, and so the idea was quickly dropped in favor of the XF4F-2, which would be a monoplane.

The prototype flew in September 1937 with a 900hp Pratt & Whitney R-1830 Twin Wasp. Comparative tests showed the F2A to be superior in most respects, at least at first. The F4F went through major airframe and engine modifications, and by the time the F4F-3 was flying, it offered much superior performance, including a top speed of 335mph at 21,000ft and a rate of climb of more than 3,000ft/min.

The Wildcat was ordered by the US Navy, while most production F2As went to air forces which were desperate for any type of modern pursuit. Most of those ordered by France were taken over by Britain's Fleet Air Arm as the Martlet I, where one of them became the first American-built pursuit to shoot down an enemy airplane when it attacked a German Ju 88.

Deliveries to the US fleet began with the F4F-4 in November 1941. These had been improved with more guns, and self-sealing fuel tanks. Several squadrons of US Marine Corps Wildcats were at Pearl Harbor when the Japanese attacked on 7 December 1941, though most were destroyed on the ground.

It wasn't until the attack on Wake Island that the Wildcat got into combat, when the remaining four succeeded in interfering dramatically with Japanese raids, and doing considerable damage to ships of the invading fleet before being overcome by sheer numbers.

While the Wildcat's star rose rapidly, its one-time rival Buffalo faded away, having shown its inability to cope with the far more maneuverable Japanese A6M Zero. Indeed, for the initial phases of the Pacific war, the Grumman was the only American carrier-based fighter, and as such scored heavily in aerial combat with Japan's best.

It wasn't until its direct descendent, the F6F Hellcat, began to replace it in early 1943 that the US Navy had a superior airplane. As production capacity was needed for the F6F, manufacture of the F4F was transferred to General Motors, where it was called the FM-1 and FM-2. Of almost 8,000 Wildcats built, nearly 6,000 came from General Motors. While none of them could claim performance superior to their opposition, they could absorb heavy battle damage and continue to fight, while the Zeros could not survive similar beatings. The Wildcat took part in all the naval battles of the early part of the war and performed brilliantly.

Specifications of the F4F-4

Length: 28ft 9in
Wingspan: 38ft 0in
Height: 9ft 3in
Wing area: 260 sq ft
Empty weight: 5,758lb
Maximum speed: 318mph at 19,400ft
Maximum range: 770 miles
Service ceiling: 39,400ft
Rate of climb: 1,950ft/min

Surviving Examples

F4F-3
BuAer 3872 – US Naval Aviation Museum
BuAer 12296 – Ford Island Museum
BuAer 12320 – Chicago O'Hare International Airport

F4F-3A
BuAer 3969 – Patriot's Point

F4F-4
BuAer 12114 – US Marine Corps Museum

FM-1
BuAer 15392 – US National Air & Space Museum
BuAer 14994 – Valiant Air Command

FM-2
BuAer 16089 and 86747 – US National Museum of Naval Aviation
BuAer 16161 – Pima Air and Space Museum
BuAer 74120 – New England Air Museum

BuAer 86581 – Kalamazoo Air Zoo
BuAer 86711 – The Fighter Collection
BuAer 86596 – Fantasy of Flight
BuAer 86774 – Planes of Fame
RN AL245 – Fleet Air Arm Museum
Civil G-RUMW – Imperial War Museum (Duxford)

Grumman F6F Hellcat

During the production run of Grumman Wildcat fighters, modifications were regularly introduced on the assembly line to improve performance and reliability, many of them as a direct result of experiences in the field. At some point, however, it became clear that there was a limit to how much an older airplane could be improved before it was time to introduce a new design. The prototype of the new F6F Hellcat first flew in July 1942, powered by the new and very promising, 2,000hp Pratt & Whitney R-2800 Double Wasp.

A major redesign of the airframe had been undertaken in order to make the best possible use of the vastly increased power. It carried six .50 cal. machine guns and could reach 380mph at 23,000ft. The first F6F-3s reached squadrons aboard the aircraft carrier USS *Essex* in January 1943, and saw their first action in August, though the airplane had entered combat with Britain's Fleet Air Arm a few weeks earlier.

Production of the F6F-3 topped 4,400, with over 200 being radar-equipped night fighters. It was then replaced on the production line by the F6F-5, having numerous improvements to the airframe, a more powerful R-2800 engine, and provisions for two 1,000lb bombs. Most had six .50 cal. machine guns, while some had four machine guns and two 20mm cannon. Total production of all versions reached 6,436 airplanes.

While the Zero retained its superiority in turning maneuvers, the F6F had superior level, climbing and diving speed, as well as general maneuverability. As soon as its pilots learned to take advantage of the airplane's superior qualities, and counter any shortcomings, the stubby fighter achieved a substantial kill-ratio over all the Japanese Navy fighters it faced.

The Hellcat was unquestionably the most important US Navy fighter of the war, and probably the most important carrier-based fighter of any of the combatants. The F6Fs were credited with more than three-quarters of all the Japanese aircraft shot down by carrier-based airplanes. Including kills by land-based Hellcats, the total was more than 5,100.

But just as the Wildcat had been replaced by the far superior Hellcat, the latter was destined to be replaced on the assembly lines by the F8F Bearcat, though too late to have any impact on the war.

Specifications of the F6F-5

Length: 33ft 7in
Wingspan: 42ft 10in
Height: 13ft 1in
Wing area: 334 sq ft
Empty weight: 9,153lb
Maximum speed: 386mph at 17,000ft
Maximum range: 1,530 miles with 150-gallon drop tank
Service ceiling: 37,300ft
Rate of climb: 3,410ft/min

Surviving Examples

F6F-3
BuAer 41476 – US Marine Corps Museum (at Evergreen Aviation),
BuAer 41930 – Chino Warbirds
BuAer 42874 – San Diego Aerospace Museum
BuAer 43014 – Fantasy of Flight

F6F-3K
BuAer 41834 – US National Air & Space Museum

F6F-5
BuAer 66237 and 94203 – National Museum of Naval Aviation
BuAer 70222 – Commemorative Air Force
BuAer 78645 – Yanks Air Museum
BuAer 79863 – Flying Heritage Collection
BuAer 93879 – Planes of Fame

F6F-5K
BuAer 77722 – US Naval Reserve at Andrews AFB
BuAer 79192 – New England Air Museum
BuAer 79593 – USS *Yorktown* at Patriots Point
BuAer 79683 – Kalamazoo Air Zoo
BuAer 80141 as '40467' – The Fighter Collection

Hellcat II
RN KE209 (BuAer 79779) – Fleet Air Arm Museum

Grumman F7F Tigercat

The US Navy had barely begun testing its first two proposed monoplane pursuits when Grumman, designer of one of them, offered up a twin-engined fighter intended for carrier operation. Not known previously for radical designs, the Long Island manufacturer wanted to build F5F Skyrockets as interceptors. The Navy, despite its well-established reputation for a conservative approach, ordered a single XF5F-1 prototype in June 1938.

Odd-looking, with its nose ending aft of the wing's leading edge, and twin vertical tails, its progress was retarded by a long string of cooling and air flow problems. The prototype's test program was not completed until early 1942, and then landing gear weaknesses set the program farther back until it was badly damaged in December 1944. Meanwhile, Grumman had modified the design into the XP-50 for the USAAF, which ordered a prototype in November 1939.

With a more conventional nose, and tricycle landing gear, it made but a single flight in May 1941, during which it was destroyed by a supercharger explosion. The follow-on XP-65 became the Navy's F7F Tigercat.

The Tigercat was a major step forward for naval aviation; it was its first production airplane with tricycle landing gear and the first such twin-engined (2,000hp Pratt & Whitney R-2800s) production airplane to operate off a carrier. With a top speed over 400mph and armament of four .50 cal. machine guns and four 20mm cannon, it was a much more lethal weapon than any of its predecessors.

The first XF7F-1 flew in December 1943, being followed quickly by an order for 500 for the US Marine Corps. In less than six months, the first F7F-1 had rolled off the assembly line. The first of the two-seat, radar-equipped F7F-2N night fighters soon followed. The F7F-3 had more powerful R-2800s, which gave it a top speed of 435mph at 22,000ft, making it the Navy's fastest piston-engined airplane.

Wartime production was just 189, none of which got into combat before V-J Day. After the war, production continued with the F7F-3N night fighter, and the similar F7F-4N. The only service to operate Tigercats in combat was the US Marines, which flew them extensively during the Korean War.

Specifications of the F7F-3

Length: 45ft 5in
Wingspan: 51ft 6in
Height: 16ft 7in
Wing area: 455 sq ft
Empty weight: 16,270lb
Maximum speed: 435mph at 22,200ft
Maximum range: 1,570 miles
Service ceiling: 40,700ft
Rate of climb: 4,530ft/min

Surviving Examples

F7F-3
BuAer 80373 – National Museum of Naval Aviation
BuAer 80404 – Fantasy of Flight
BuAer 80410 – Pima Air and Space Museum
BuAer 80412 – Palm Springs Air Museum

F7F-3N
BuAer 80375 – Pima Air and Space Museum
BuAer 80382 – Planes of Fame
BuAer 80503 – racing as #1 'Big Bossman'

F7F-3P
BuAer 80390 – Kalamazoo Air Zoo
BuAer 80425 – The Fighter Collection

Grumman F8F Bearcat

The final step in the long line of piston-engined US Navy fighters by Grumman, it was also the last such fighter built for the Navy. A direct descendent of the Wildcat and Hellcat, it was the smallest airframe that could contain the potent Pratt & Whitney R-2800 and sufficient fuel, along with someone to steer it. Compared with the F6F, it was considerably smaller and lighter, and thus almost 50mph faster.

Intended for low-altitude combat in the Pacific, it would certainly have had a major impact had the war continued. But when the last shot was fired, the first Bearcat squadrons were still being prepared for deployment. As it turned out, the airplane would never see combat with US forces, though the French flew them in Indo-China, and many were sent to Thailand for its air force.

More than 2,000 F8F-1s had been ordered from Grumman, and another 1,875 as F3M-1s from General Motors' Eastern Aircraft Division. All of the latter and most of the former were cancelled at the end of the war.

After the war, Grumman built more than a thousand additional Bearcats. This included 100 F8F-1B, 36 F8F-1N night fighters, 293 F8F-2 with enlarged vertical tails to correct a stability problem, 12 F8F-2N night fighters and 60 F8F-2P photo-reconnaissance airplanes. All future Grumman fighters would be jets.

Specifications of the F8F-2

Length: 28ft 3in
Wingspan: 35ft 10in
Height: 13ft 10in
Wing area: 244 sq ft
Empty weight: 7,070lb
Maximum speed: 421mph at 19,700ft
Maximum range: 1,965 miles with two 150-gallon drop tanks
Service ceiling: 38,700ft
Rate of climb: 4,570ft/min

Surviving Examples

XF8F-1
BuAer 90446 – raced as #14 by owner Howard Pardue

F8F-1
BuAer 90454 – Kalamazoo Air Zoo
BuAer 94956 – Royal Thai Museum

F8F-1B
one privately owned

F8F-2
BuAer 121646 – US National Air & Space Museum (ex-#1 Darryl Greenamyer 3 km record)

BuAer 121710 – National Museum of Naval Aviation
BuAer 122629 – #77 racer 'Rare Bear'

F8F-2P
BuAer 21714 – The Fighter Collection
BuAer 122674 – Commemorative Air Force

Civil G-58B
c/n D.1262 – Planes of Fame

McDonnell FH-1 Phantom I

The first airplane built by the new McDonnell Aircraft Company was the P-67 'Bat', a twin-engined machine of somewhat unusual blended wing-fuselage design which failed to attract an Army contract. The second was the FD-1 (later the FH-1) Phantom (later called the Phantom I), which became the US Navy's first pure jet fighter to operate off a carrier.

After considering powering the new design with as many as eight very small jet engines, McDonnell settled on a pair of Westinghouse 1,600lb units tucked into the wing roots. The XFD-1 made its first test flight on 26 January 1945 with only one engine installed, and this was soon followed by an order for 100 airplanes. When the war ended, 40 of those were cancelled, one of the remaining ones becoming the first American jet to land on a carrier, in July 1946.

Deliveries of the Phantom I began to US Marine Corps units in January 1947, with most of those soon relegated to training roles. The Navy learned a lot about operating jets from carriers, but with a top speed of under 500mph, the Phantom I could not hold its own with contemporary rivals.

Specifications of the FH-1

Length: 37ft 3in
Wingspan: 40ft 9in
Height: 14ft 2in
Wing area: 276 sq ft
Empty weight: 6,155lb
Maximum speed: 487mph at sea level
Maximum range: 750 miles
Service ceiling: 43,700ft
Rate of climb: 4,950 ft/min

Surviving Examples

FH-1
BuAer 111759 – US National Air & Space Museum
BuAer 111768 – US Marine Corps Museum

Ryan FR Fireball

Frustrated by the inability of the first turbojet engines to get a modern jet fighter off the ground quickly and also to enable a jet fighter to have a reasonable range, engineers tried mixed-power airplanes which had both a piston engine and a turbojet engine. The first of these was the Ryan FR-1 Fireball.

Three prototypes and 100 production FR-1s were ordered as early as December 1943, with one flying the following June. Power was supplied by a 1,350hp Wright ER-1820 and a 1,600lb General Electric J31 jet engine. It achieved 425mph at 18,000ft on both engines, and 400mph at sea level on the piston engine alone. It had a fully flush-riveted airframe and a laminar flow airfoil similar to that of the P-51 Mustang.

In January 1945, 1,000 more Fireballs were ordered, suggesting the Navy was more than satisfied with its performance and flying characteristics. The first squadron was formed and began preparations for action. Before the type could enter combat, however, the war ended, and 1,044 of the 1,100 that had been ordered were cancelled. Among those completed were the XFR-2, which had an uprated Wright engine and a much more powerful Westinghouse turbojet.

By then, however, interest was waning in mixed-power airplanes, as the power output of jet engines was rising rapidly, and the next generation of pure jets was expected to reduce, if not solve the problems for which airplanes like the Fireball had been created. This was the first and last combat airplane to be built by the company that had come to fame in 1927 with the 'Spirit of St. Louis' in which Charles Lindbergh had become the first to fly solo across the Atlantic Ocean. Ryan's future lay in jet-powered target drones and then UAVs.

Specifications of the FR-1

Length: 32ft 4in
Wingspan: 40ft 0in
Height: 13ft 7in
Wing area: 275 sq ft
Empty weight: 7,915lb
Maximum speed: 426mph at sea level
Maximum range: 1,430 miles with one 150-gallon drop tank
Service ceiling: 43,100ft
Rate of climb: 4,800ft/min

Surviving Example

FR-1
BuAer 39709 – Planes of Fame

Vought F4U Corsair

It was one of the first two American fighters to exceed 400mph in level flight, and was generally considered the finest all-round naval fighter of the war, though its operations from aircraft carriers were limited and began late in the war.

Its distinctive gull-shaped wings were designed to permit the landing gear struts to be short enough to retract into the available space inside the wings, while keeping the tips of the very large propeller from hitting the ground. The shape also enabled the wings to intersect the fuselage at close to a 90 degree angle, considered optimum for low drag.

The first Corsair – an XF4U-1 – flew on 29 May 1940, more than a year and a half before the United States entered the war. It had an 18-cylinder, 1,800hp Pratt & Whitney R-2800 Double Wasp engine. The design was accepted by the Navy in late February 1941, and large-scale production orders followed quickly.

The entry into service came in February 1943, over Guadalcanal in the South Pacific, when Marine Corps pilots operated them from runways hurriedly scraped out of the dense jungle. The Navy's standard Grumman F4F Wildcats were being out-performed by Japanese Mitsubishi A6M Zeros, and so the new airplanes were greeted with great enthusiasm, at least by the Allies. When compared with the best Japanese fighters, the Corsair had superior firepower, speed and ability to absorb punishment.

The F4U-4 version, with a semi-bubble canopy and a more powerful version of the R-2800 engine, made its debut in late 1944. It was eventually approved for carrier use despite its high landing speed and poor forward visibility. It was unquestionably the finest carrier-based fighter of the war, though the Grumman F8F Bearcat would probably have been better had it been ready in time to see action.

Total production during the war was 10,757, with many more rolling off the production lines as late as 1953 for use in the Korean conflict. More than 6,000 were built by Chance Vought as F4Us, along with 4,000 by Goodyear as FG-1s, and a few by Brewster as F3As.

The Corsair was the final American propeller-driven fighter in production, and the final type to serve on active duty. The F2G-1 version, powered by a 4,000hp Pratt & Whitney R-4360 Wasp Major, was designed to intercept Japanese kamikaze suicide planes, but never progressed beyond experimental status. It made its name in the late 1940s in the Cleveland National Air Races' featured Thompson Trophy Race.

Specifications of the F4U-4

Length: 33ft 8in
Wingspan: 40ft 11in
Height: 14ft 9in
Wing area: 314 sq ft
Empty weight: 9,205lb
Maximum speed: 446mph at 26,200ft
Maximum range: 1,560 miles
Service ceiling: 41,500ft
Rate of climb: 3,870ft/min

Surviving Examples

F4U-1A
BuAer 17799 – Planes of Fame
BuAer 17995 – Wings of Dreams

F4U-1D
BuAer 50375 – US National Museum of Naval Aviation (as an F4U-1A)
FAA KD345 – Imperial War Museum (Duxford)

XF4U-4
BuAer 80759 – New England Air Museum

F4U-4
BuAer 97259 – EAA Museum
BuAer 97349 – USMC, at Pima Air and Space Museum

BuAer 97142 – US Naval Aviation Museum
BuAer 81698 – War Eagles Air Museum
BuAer 97286 – Fantasy of Flight
BuAer 97369 – US Marine Corps Museum

F4U-4B
Wilmington, Delaware

FG-1
BuAer 13459 – US Marine Corps Museum

FG-1D
BuAer 92013 and 92246 – US National Naval Aviation Museum
BuAer 88086 – Fantasy of Flight
BuAer 88297 – The Fighter Collection
BuAer 88382 – Museum of Flight (Seattle)
BuAer 92460 – Sikorsky Memorial Airport
BuAer 92506 – Kalamazoo Air Zoo

F3A-1
Lex Cralley, Minnesota

Corsair Mk.IV
RN KD431 (BuAer 14862) – Fleet Air Arm Museum

F2G-1
BuAer 88458 – flying as race #57 in La Canada, California

F2G-1D
BuAer 88454 – Museum of Flight (Seattle)

F2G-2
BuAer 88463 – Under restoration as 1940s racer #74

Chapter Three

Great Britain

Boulton Paul Defiant

The idea of a fighter with moveable guns operated by a second crew member dates back to World War One and airplanes like the Bristol Fighter. They worked fairly well in that war and so the British continued the practice. The advantage, at least at first, was that a gunner could move his weapons in different directions, while fixed guns could only move as the airplane changed its heading.

Hawker Demons, many of which had power-operated turrets, rather than hand-aimed guns, were in RAF service from 1933 until shortly before World War Two. Boulton Paul, which had been building Demons on license, then designed its own monoplane fighter, called the Defiant. The first of these flew in August 1937 and bore more than a slight resemblance to the Hurricane.

Despite having a 1,000hp Rolls-Royce Merlin for power, its top speed was barely 300mph. It was felt, however, that the turret would be enough of a surprise to enemy pilots that this would compensate at least partly for the lower speed. The prototype flew in May 1939, and Mk.I production airplanes were rolling off the assembly line two months later.

The drawbacks of the new airplane became immediately apparent. Weighing almost a ton more than a Hurricane, it had both an inferior rate of climb and more limited combat maneuverability. It was obvious, too, that while it might score well the first time it met German airplanes, its source of surprise could hardly be kept secret, and henceforth it would be at a considerable disadvantage.

A Defiant scored its first kill – a Ju 88 – in May 1940, and the next day a flight of them engaged some Ju 87 Stuka dive bombers, claiming four shot down. They were then set upon by Messerschmitt Bf 109Es, which promptly shot down five of the six Defiants. Amazingly, the era of surprise continued. In late May they were sent to cover the evacuation of the British Army from Dunkirk, France, and their pilots claimed more than 50 German airplanes shot down, though this highly optimistic figure was later considerably reduced.

The squadron commander explained this unexpected success as the result of the Germans thinking they had encountered Hurricanes, which of course had no moveable guns. Regardless, the Germans did not repeat their mistake, and were soon taking advantage of the Defiant's lack of performance with the result that all of them were pulled out of combat in July 1940. An effort to convert the Defiant into a night fighter was initially successful, thanks to its airborne radar, and at least 25 squadrons were so equipped.

Defiants were used at night until the middle of 1943, when specially developed airplanes took over their 'temporary' duties. They then assumed air-sea rescue functions, replacing Westland Lysanders and carrying two small droppable dinghies. The final use for the one-time fighter was for towing aerial targets for student gunners.

The Boulton Paul airplane was a failure in its original purpose, but under the pressure of war, found other ways to make its contribution.

Specifications of the Defiant F Mk.I

Length: 35ft 4in
Wingspan: 39ft 4in
Height: 11ft 4in
Wing area: 250 sq ft
Empty weight: 6,080lb
Maximum speed: 304mph at 17,000ft
Maximum range: 465 miles
Service ceiling: 30,350ft
Rate of climb: 1,900 ft/min

Surviving Example

F Mk.I
RAF N1671 – RAF Museum (Hendon)

Bristol Beaufighter

Ground-based radar, used for tracking incoming enemy aircraft, was in use as World War Two began. Its aerial counterpart – Airborne Intercept (AI) radar – would be the next major step in the rapidly developing technology, and led to the first effective night fighters by providing the crew with 'eyes' to see in the dark.

The first night fighter with both its own radar and enough speed to catch German bombers was the Beaufighter, initially composed of a Bristol Beaufort torpedo bomber airframe with a new front fuselage and more powerful Bristol Hercules radial engines. The prototype flew in July 1939, followed by the first production Mk.IF in February 1941. They entered squadron service as night fighters in September 1940, and scored their first kills in November.

The 'Beau' was a major advancement from the radar-less single-engined fighters that had depended on ground controllers for generalized, rather than highly specific information. Suddenly, they could follow their own radar, much to the dismay of German pilots who had been marauding at will.

Specially equipped and armed Beaufighters then began operating as long-range day fighters in the African desert at about the same time, and then in the Mediterranean in May 1941. Also in the spring of 1941, they began to replace Bristol Blenheims in the role of Coastal Command long-range fighters, becoming highly affective in attacking enemy shipping with air-launched torpedoes.

Beaufighters used a variety of engines, some merely in tests, and others in production. Most were powered by the air-cooled, 14-cylinder sleeve-valve Bristol Hercules, which started out producing 1,300hp and was eventually developed into the Mk.XVII with almost 1,800hp. Corresponding increases in performance were not realized, however, as the later model airplanes were considerably heavier, with more fuel, armament and radar equipment.

Starting with the Mk.II Beaufighter, the shortage of radial engines led to the installation of the Rolls-Royce Merlin V-12. While the top speed did increase, the reduced area ahead of the center of gravity necessitated the addition of a large dorsal fin ahead of the vertical tail and a this resulted in a very different profile.

Armament varied just as widely, with the early Mk.IF carrying four 20mm cannon in its nose and six .30 cal. machine guns in its wings. One prototype had the four cannon replaced by a pair of 40mm guns. A version that never went into production had the same selection of guns, plus a top turret with four more .30 cal. machine guns. The Mk. IVc was the first designed to carry a full-size torpedo, making it one of the finest anti-shipping fighter-bombers of the war.

By the time the war ended, the Beaufighter had been active in every theater of war, thanks to a total production run of almost 6,000, of which some 360 were built in Australia. It was one of the few foreign-design airplanes to be used in large numbers by the USAAF, which operated more than 100 as night fighters.

The immediate successor to the Beaufighter was the early post-war Brigand, a somewhat larger, heavier and more powerful fighter-bomber which, like the Beaufighter, was developed from a light bomber, in this case the lesser-known Buckingham.

Specifications of the Beaufighter TF Mk.X

Length: 41ft 8in
Wingspan: 57ft 10in
Height: 15ft 10in
Wing area: 503 sq ft
Empty weight: 15,600lb

Maximum speed: 303mph at 13,000ft
Maximum range: 1,800 miles with auxiliary tanks
Service ceiling: 15000ft
Rate of climb:

Surviving Examples

TF Mk.X
RAF RD253 – RAF Museum (Hendon)
RAF RD867 – Canadian National Air Museum

F Mk.21
RAF JM135 – The Fighter Collection
RAAF A8-186 – Camden (Australia) Museum of Aviation
RAAF A19-43 – National Museum of the US Air Force

de Havilland DH.100 Vampire

The Vampire was developed in parallel with the Meteor, much as the Spitfire had been paired with the Hurricane. The design differences were considerably greater, however, the Vampire having a single jet engine in a twin-boom layout. It had three feet shorter wingspan, 10 feet shorter length and weighed 2,800lb less.

The Vampire saw the first light of day on drawing boards in 1941, in response to a government requirement. The unusual layout was chosen to reduce the power losses due to long tailpipes in other jets. Power for all but the earliest Vampires was supplied by a single de Havilland Goblin II, whose 3,100lb of thrust almost equaled the two engines of the early Meteors. Like the Meteor, it was armed with four 20mm cannon.

The first prototype Vampire flew six months after the Meteor, but while the latter was the chosen vehicle for the upgrading of Britain's Fighter Command, the first production Vampire wasn't completed until a few days after Meteors began operations from advanced bases in liberated Western Europe. No Vampire was directly involved in the war.

By the end of production in 1950, some 4,000 had been built, including night fighters and two-seat trainers. Direct developments of the original Vampire included the Sea Vampire, the Venom, the carrier-based Sea Venom and the Royal Navy's Sea Vixen all-weather fighter that served into the 1970s.

Specifications of the Vampire F Mk.I

Length: 30ft 9in
Wingspan: 40ft 0in
Height: 8ft 10in
Wing area: 266 sq ft
Empty weight: 6,370lb
Maximum speed: 530mph at 17,500ft
Maximum range: 1,145 miles with two 120-gallon drop tanks
Service ceiling: 42,800 ft
Rate of climb: 4,200ft/min

Surviving Examples

F Mk.I
RAF TG372 – Canadian National Air Museum

F Mk.3
RAF VT812 – RAF Museum (Hendon)

RCAF 17074 – Canadian National Air Museum
Planes of Fame

Sea Vampire
FAA LZ551/G – Fleet Air Arm Museum

de Havilland DH.98 Mosquito

It was not unusual for an airplane to assume duties not originally envisioned by its manufacturers or designers, such as USAAF P-38s, P-47s and P-51s receiving bomb shackles and becoming fighter-bombers. It was much less common for an airplane intended to be a bomber to become an effective fighter, as did the Mosquito. The Mosquito was probably the most versatile airplane of World War

Two, with roughly half being built as bombers, half as fighters and many others as photo-reconnaissance airplanes.

Inspiration for the Mosquito came from the Albatross, de Havilland's unusually clean, four-engined 1937 airliner. The Mosquito fighter prototype was designed, built and tested at Salisbury Hall, a 17th Century estate north of London that now houses the de Havilland Heritage Museum. The first Mosquito – the bomber prototype – flew in November 1940, while the fighter prototype flew from Salisbury Hall six months later, to be followed after just a few weeks by the prototype of the photo-reconnaissance version.

The original plan was to build a bomber that was so fast that it could not be intercepted by enemy fighters and thus would need no defensive armament. It was to be built almost entirely of non-strategic materials, meaning wood. With no need for extensive tooling, it could be built quickly by small wood shops dispersed around the country instead of huge factories which provided such good targets for enemy bombers.

When the bomber prototype demonstrated speed close to 400mph, along with maneuverability previously unknown for a bomber (it could perform vertical rolls on one engine), the widespread lack of enthusiasm for an 'old fashioned' wooden bomber lacking gun turrets dissolved. The initial order was for more fighters than bombers, with the F Mk.I carrying four 20mm cannon and four .30 cal. machine guns in fixed mountings in the nose.

The first action seen by any version was in September 1941, when barely three months after the PR prototype had flown, one of the first built outran three Messerschmitt Bf 109s bent on interception and successfully photographed its French target in broad daylight.

effective against ships when used in conjunction with 500lb bombs or 60lb unguided air-to-surface rockets.

The achievements of Mosquitos are legendary. They were used to shoot down more than 400 V-1 buzz-bombs which could fly at 400mph, and they attacked the Gestapo prison in Amiens, France, wrecking the building and allowing more than 250 members of the French Resistance to escape. Other pin-point bombing attacks were made on a Gestapo administrative center, destroying records of the Dutch and Danish resistance and saving untold hundreds of lives.

Specifications of the Mosquito

Length: 40ft 11in
Wingspan: 54ft 2in
Height: 15ft 4in
Wing area: 454 sq ft
Empty weight: 15,400lb
Maximum speed: 407mph at 28,000ft
Maximum range: 1,300 miles at 250mph
Service ceiling: 39,000ft

Surviving Examples

FB Mk.VI
RAF TA122 – de Havilland Heritage Museum

NF Mk.II
RAF 'HJ711' – Yorkshire Air Museum

The great need at this time was for a radar-equipped night fighter that could deal with Lutwaffe Heinkel He 111s and Junkers Ju 88s routinely bombing London and targets in many parts of England. In May 1942, the Mosquito NF Mk.II entered service. On the power of a pair of 1,450hp Rolls-Royce Merlin V-12s, it was as fast as the early Spitfires and Hurricanes even while carrying the weighty specialized equipment required for night fighting.

Success in combat with early versions of the Mosquito was followed by the FB Mk.IV, a fighter-bomber produced in greater numbers than any other. The first one – a modified Mk.II – flew in February 1943, and saw its first action in May of that year. The follow-on FB Mk.XVIII carried the standard four machine gun armament, plus a 57mm cannon mounted just under the nose and replacing the four 20mm cannon. This was found to be highly

Fairey Firefly

It began with the Fairey Fulmar, the first heavily-armed monoplane fighter to serve with the Royal Navy, which flew for the first time in January 1940. It, in turn, was a development of the RAF's Fairey Battle light bomber of 1937. The Fulmar was powered by a 1,100hp Rolls-Royce Merlin V-12 and carried eight .303 cal. machine guns. It entered squadron service in July 1940, and had its first combat against the Italians in August 1940. Production ended in early 1943.

The Firefly, visually very similar to the Fulmar, flew in December 1941, with a 1,730hp Rolls-Royce Griffon V-12 engine, then in an early stage of development. It didn't enter operations until the summer of 1944, when it was used against German shipping off Norway, where its four 20mm cannon, the heaviest armament yet carried by a British carrier-based airplane, stood it in good stead.

Total production of the F Mk.I was 429, and was followed by the FR Mk.I – a fighter/reconnaissance version equipped with radar – of which 376 were built through 1946. It was followed by the FR Mk.IV, which flew in May 1945, powered by a 2,300hp Rolls-Royce Griffon 72. Production of the Mk.I Firefly totaled 375 and continued until late 1946, while the Mk.IV, which had a Griffon engine, was built through 1947.

Specifications of the Firefly FR Mk.IV

Length: 37ft 11in
Wingspan: 41ft 2in
Height: 14ft 4in
Wing area: 330 sq ft
Empty weight: 9,675lb
Maximum speed: 386mph at 14,000ft
Maximum range: 1,300 miles with drop tanks
Service ceiling: 28,800ft
Rate of climb: 7:09 to 10,000ft

Surviving Examples

F Mk.1
FAA Z2033 – Fleet Air Arm Museum

FR Mk.1
RAF R7384 – Canadian National Aviation Museum

FB Mk.1
RN MB410 – Royal Thai Aviation Museum
FAA MB210 – Fleet Air Arm Museum

TT Mk.1
RN PP392 – Swedish Air Force Museum

TT Mk.4
FAA VH127 – Fleet Air Arm Museum

TT Mk.5
RAN WD826 – Australian Naval Air Museum

AS Mk.6
FAA WH632 – Canadian Warplane Heritage
privately owned, Rockport, Maine

Gloster Gladiator

As a mid-1930s biplane pursuit, the Gladiator was one of the best. As a late 1930s fighter, it was obsolete before the first one joined the Royal Air Force. When the war started, more than one-third of the RAF's fighter squadrons were still equipped with Gladiators, though most of them would soon receive their first Hurricanes and Spitfires.

It was the direct descendant of the Gauntlet, the last of the RAF's open-cockpit fighters and, until 1937, was the RAF's fastest fighter.

When the British Army shipped out to France as World War Two began, it was accompanied by two RAF Auxiliary squadrons with their Gladiators. No match for Germany's Messerschmitts, the few remaining ones were quickly grounded. Another squadron supported British troops sent to Norway in April 1940; the few surviving airplanes and most of their pilots were lost when the ship evacuating them was sunk.

But still they soldiered on. Their finest hour came in June when a few heavily outnumbered Gladiators fought off the Italian Air Force's attacks on the little island of Malta for more than two weeks until reinforcements arrived, in the shape of Hawker Hurricanes. In late 1940, they were again in action, this time in Greece, and later fought the Italians in the Western Desert.

The first Sea Gladiators were RAF Gladiator IIs modified with arrestor hooks and catapult connections, while others were built expressly for carrier operations, seeing action in the Mediterranean and the North Sea. These were retired in favor of Lend-Lease Grumman F4Fs in late 1940. The RAF retired its last in 1941.

Importing countries included Latvia and Lithuania as well as China, where they were highly successful against the Japanese. Twenty-two were ordered by Belgium, and 55 by Sweden, many of those going to Finland, where as types J8 and L8A, they were flown against the Soviets. A dozen went to Norway, 15 to Iraq, others to Eire, Portugal amd Greece. Total production reached 527, a large number for that period.

Specifications of the Gladiator Mk.I

Length: 27ft 5in
Wingspan: 32ft 3in
Height: 10ft 4in
Wing area: 323 sq ft
Empty weight: 3,475lb
Maximum speed: 253mph at 14,500ft
Maximum range: 410 miles
Service ceiling: 33,000ft
Rate of climb: 2,350ft/min

Surviving Examples

Mk.I
L8032 –Shuttleworth Collection

Sea Gladiator Mk.I
RN N5519 – National War Museum, Malta

Mk.II
RAF N5641 – Armed Forces Museum, Oslo
RAF K8042 – RAF Museum (Hendon)
RAF N5641 – Royal Norwegian Air Force Museum
RAF N5903 – The Fighter Collection

J.8A
Royal Swedish AF Fv278 – Flygvapenmuseum, Sweden

Gloster Meteor

The most important technical advance in aviation during World War Two was almost certainly the turbojet engine and the airplanes that used it to reach previously unheard of speeds. Britain's development of this novel power plant began in 1928 with Frank Whittle's theoretical work and became hardware in 1937 when he ran the world's first turbojet engine intended for aircraft propulsion. In May 1941, Gloster flew its E.28/39 research airplane with the Whittle engine, making it the first non-German jet to fly.

In September 1941, the first production order, for 20 airplanes, was signed, long before the first Meteor (at first called the Thunderbolt) had flown. On 5 March 1943, an F.9/40 prototype of the Gloster Meteor flew on the power of two Halford H.1 engines, rated at 1,500lb of thrust. Spurred on by reports of Messerschmitt Me 262s in combat as early as June 1944, the Meteor was sent into action.

In late July 1944, the first jet-v-jet combat took place when a Meteor pilot shot down a pilotless V-1 buzz-bomb by slipping his wingtip under the V-1, then rolling quickly and tipping it over, thus causing its gyro to tumble and the V-1 to go out of control and crash. Later in the day, a second V-1 was shot down, this time by a Meteor's four 20mm cannon.

By August a full squadron had been equipped with Meteors and had been credited with shooting down more than a dozen V-1s, by which time the flying bomb launch sites had been occupied by Allied troops. In January 1945, a Meteor squadron was stationed in liberated Belgium, the first overseas deployment of a jet fighter, and went into action a short time later. These were Mk.IIs, most of them powered by 2,000lb Rolls-Royce Derwent engines, which raised their top speed from 410mph to almost 500mph. The war in Europe ended in May 1945, before there could be any air-to-air combat with the few Me 262s left.

Specifications of the Meteor Mk.III

Length: 41ft 3in
Wingspan: 43ft 0in
Height: 13ft 0in
Wing area: 374 sq ft
Empty weight: 8,810lb
Maximum speed: 493mph at 30,000ft
Maximum range: 1,340 miles at 350mph at 30,000ft
Service ceiling: 44,000ft
Rate of climb: 3,980ft/min

On 7 November 1945, Group Capt H J Wilson flew a Meteor F.4 to an official World Speed Record of 606mph, topping the 469mph achieved by an experimental development of the Bf 109 called the Me 209. Later, another Meteor raised the record to 616mph; to increase its speed, the wings were clipped from 43ft to 37ft. The reduction proved so successful that subsequent production airplanes were similarly modified.

Almost 3,900 were built in Britain and under license by Fokker in the Netherlands before production ceased in 1954. Meteors remained in service with the Royal Air Force until 1961, their duties by then having included research (on ejection seats and even the prone pilot position), and finally target-towing. There was no direct follow-on to the Meteor, as Gloster's next combat airplane, the Javelin all-weather fighter of the early 1950s, bore it no obvious resemblance.

Surviving Examples

F.9/40
RAF DG202/G – RAF Museum (Cosford)

F Mk.IV
RAF VT229 – Fantasy of Flight
RAF VT260 – Planes of Fame

T Mk.VII
RAF WA634 – RAF Museum (Cosford)
FAA WS103 – Fleet Air Arm Museum

F Mk.VIII
RAF WH301 – RAF Museum (Hendon)

F Mk.8 prone pilot
RAF WK935 — RAF Museum(Cosford)

Hawker Demon

Military airplane design in the early 1930s was in a state of flux, with new bombers demonstrating their ability to outrun operational fighters. In America, the Martin B-10 was faster than any Army or Navy fighter, while in Britain, the Hawker Hart day bomber entered service in January 1930, as the fastest airplane in RAF service.

To correct the embarrassing imbalance and to take advantage of the Hart's superior performance, one Hart was converted into a two-seat fighter with a 485hp Rolls-Royce Kestrel V-12 engine. This was a continuation of a World War One practice for a fighter

with two fixed forward-firing Vickers machine guns and a rear gunner with a moveable Lewis machine gun. Only the Bristol F2B had performed up to expectations, and then only if the serious discomfort of the gunner during dogfights was ignored.

The newly renamed Demon entered service in a test program, equipping one squadron that also retained its Bristol Bulldogs, just in case the new airplane disappointed. In 1933, the Demon won over enough of the doubters, and production plans called for 79 airplanes with the Kestrel IIS, which was soon superseded by the 585hp Kestrel V. Total production reached 234, of which almost half were built by Boulton Paul. Most of the latter had the World War One-style gunner's position replaced by a power turret. Another 77

with the larger engine were built for the Australians, where many of them were fitted out for ground-support duties with provisions for eight 20lb bombs.

In 1935, two RAF squadrons of Demons reinforced RAF units during the Abyssinian (Ethiopian) crisis. Two other squadrons operated in the Mediterranean, while still others served with RAF Auxiliary squadrons. By the approach of war, every Demon had been retired from front-line use and assigned duties as target tugs upon being replaced as night fighters by Bristol Blenheims.

Specifications of the Demon Mk.I

Length: 29ft 7in
Wingspan: 37ft 3in
Height: 10ft 5in
Wing area: 348 sq ft
Empty weight: 3,067lb
Maximum speed: 182mph at 13,000ft
Maximum Range: 375 miles
Service ceiling: 27,500ft
Rate of climb: 3,280ft in 2:06

Surviving Examples

RAF K8203 – Shuttleworth Collection
RAAF A1-8 – Royal Australian Air Force Museum

Hawker Hurricane

Clearly overshadowed by the more glamorous Spitfire, the Hurricane was there when it was needed most: the Battle of Britain.

Here it shot down more enemy airplanes than any other type of British fighter. Its simpler structure enabled more of them to be built quickly when the demand for fighters in quantity was at its peak.

Hawker's experience in building fighters was unsurpassed. Starting with the 138mph Woodcock in 1924, it progressed through the Fury I in 1930 to the Demon of 1932 to the Fury II of 1937. When viewed from the side, the fuselage of the latter bears an unmistakable similarity to that of the Hurricane.

What eventually became the Hurricane started out as the Fury Monoplane in 1933 and became the Interceptor Monoplane upon the emergence of the Rolls-Royce V-12 Merlin engine. The first prototype flew in December 1935, followed by the first production Mk.I in October 1937. Despite its wooden, fixed-pitch, two-bladed

propeller, it could climb at 2,400ft/min and reach 320mph, which was 70mph faster than the Gloster Gladiator, the final and fastest RAF biplane fighter.

By the time the Battle of Britain began, 2,300 Hurricanes had been delivered, and 32 squadrons were flying them, as against 1,400 Spitfires in 19 squadrons. Together, there were 3,700 modern fighters ready to face the enemy.

While Hurricanes were being churned out by the thousands, Hawker was already hard at work on its replacements. The Tornado, powered by a 2,000hp Rolls-Royce Vulture X-24 engine, flew in October 1939 and was capable of almost 400mph. Serious problems with the engine led to it being cancelled, and with it the Tornado. Barely four months later, the prototype Typhoon flew; despite problems with its 2,300hp Napier Sabre H-24 engine, it went into production. In early 1943, the Tempest flew, powered by the same engine, whose eventual cancellation spelled *finis* to the Mk.I, though by then the Mk.II, powered by a 2,500hp Bristol Centaurus sleeve-valve radial engine, was undergoing flight tests.

Despite the superior performance of newer designs, the Hurricane remained in full-scale production, having proven itself highly adaptable to new demands. The Mk.II used two different wings: one with twelve .30 cal. machine guns (IIB), and one with four 20mm cannon (IIC), while both could carry up to 1,000lb of bombs in its 'Hurribomber' guise. The Mk.IIC became the first single-seat fighter to be armed with air-to-ground rockets. The later Mk.IID carried the unusual armament of two 40mm cannon, and became a major weapon against Rommel's tanks in North Africa.

Additional production of the Hurricane was established in Canada. The Canadian-built Mk.X was the same as the Mk.IIB, while the Mks.XII and XIIA were powered by Packard-built Rolls-Royce engines. In all, more than 1,400 were built in Canada. Some of these, along with more built by Hawker, were Sea Hurricanes, modified for use on small carriers which accompanied convoys of freighters and troop ships across the Atlantic. In all, 14,233 Hurricanes were built.

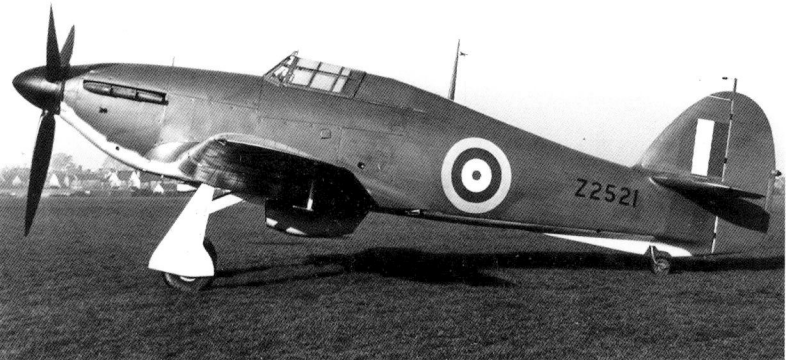

Specifications of the Hurricane Mk.IIC

Length: 32ft 3in
Wingspan: 40ft 0in
Height: 8ft 9in
Wing area: 258 sq ft
Empty weight: 5,800lb
Maximum speed: 342mph at 22,000ft
Maximum range: 970 miles
Service ceiling: 35,600ft
Rate of climb:

Surviving Examples

Mk.I
RAF L1592 – Science Museum (London)
RAF P2617 – RAF Museum (Hendon)

RAF N2394 – Air Museum of Central Finland
RAF AE977 – Planes of Fame

Mk.IIB
RAF AB832 – Indian Air Force Museum
RAF 'BE421' – RAF Museum (Hendon)
'RCAF 5390' – National Museum of the US Air Force

Mk.IIC
RAF LF658 ('LF345') – Royal Army Museum, Brussels
RAF LD619 – South African Museum of Military History
RAF LF363 and PZ865 – Battle of Britain Memorial Flight
RAF LF686 – US National Air & Space Museum
RAF LF736 – RAF Museum (Cosford)

Mk.IV
RAF KZ321 – The Fighter Collection
RAF LD975 – Yugoslav Air Museum

Mk.XII
RCAF 5584 – Canadian National Aviation Museum
RCAF 5711 – Historic Aircraft Collection
RCAF '5390' – National Museum of the US Air Force
RCAF 5400 – Fantasy of Flight
RCAF 5667 – Fighter Factory

Mk.XIIA
RCAF BW881 – Flying Heritage Collection

Sea Hurricane Ib
FAA KZ321 – Shuttleworth Collection

Hawker Sea Fury

It was the last piston-engined fighter to be produced in quantity by any industrial nation, and the last of the long line of Hawker fighters dating back to the Fury I of 1931. It began with the study of a pristine Focke Wulf FW 190 which an obviously confused Luftwaffe pilot had landed at an RAF base in England in 1942.

By bolting the outer wings of a Hawker Tempest together, without the Tempest's center section, the first Fury came out smaller and lighter, but with a late-model, 2,400hp Bristol Centaurus sleeve-valve radial engine. Standard armament was four 20mm cannon, plus as much as 2,000lb of bombs and rockets.

Both the Royal Air Force and the Royal Navy were interested in the design, with the prototype land-based, Centaurus-powered Fury making its first flight on 1 September 1944, while the second, with a Rolls-Royce Griffon V-12 and contra-rotating propellers, flew in February 1945. In May 1945, that airplane flew with a 3,000hp Napier Sabre engine, achieving the highest top speed of any version: 485mph at 18,500 feet. The navalized Sea Fury, with folding wings and an arrestor hook, made its first flight on 21 February 1945. All 100 original production airplanes – each a Sea Fury – were completed after the end of the war, following cancellation of orders for 300 more.

Post-war production totaled 860, with many going to the Netherlands, West Germany, Egypt, Canada, Cuba, Australia, Iraq and Burma. Sixty were two-seat T.20s used for training as target tugs, mainly by Germany. The Royal Navy operated them during the Korean conflict from aircraft carriers until replaced by jets around 1953.

Many of the surviving Sea Furys can be seen each September during the National Championship Air Races at Reno, Nevada.

Most of the 20 that have raced there have been FB.11s, with the majority of those having been modified with more powerful engines (e.g. Wright R-3350 and Pratt & Whitney R-4360) and varying degrees of airframe modifications and clean-up. Despite the obvious visual changes, many of them are still displayed in authentic military colors and markings.

Specifications of the Sea Fury

Length: 34ft 7in
Wingspan: 38ft 5in
Height: 14ft 8in
Wing area: 285 sq ft
Empty weight: 8,615lb
Maximum speed: 435mph at 18,500ft
Maximum range: 1,480 miles with two 45-gallon drop tanks
Service ceiling: 43,500ft
Rate of climb: 4,300ft/min

Surviving Examples

F.10 Baghdad Fury
c/n 37703 (ISS25) – War Eagles Air Museum
c/n 37536 (ISS25) – Howard Pardue, Breckenridge, Texas.

FB.11
FAA WJ231 – Fleet Air Arm Museum
FAA VW263 – Royal Navy Historic Flight
FAA TG119 – Canadian National Museum
FAA TG114 – racing as #232 'September Fury' (R-3350)
FAA WG567 – racing as #87 'Miss Merced' (R-3350)

FAA VW232 – Australian War Memorial
FAA WG652 – racing as #99 'Riff Raff' (R-3350)
FAA WG599 – Luftwaffe Museum

T.20
FAA VZ368 – racing as #8 'Dreadnought', Sanders Aircraft, Ione, California (R-4360)
FAA VX351 – racing as #911 'September Pops'
FAA WE280 – racing as #1 'Critical Mass'

Hawker Tempest

The immediate successor to the Typhoon – the Tempest – was clearly related, despite major differences. Originally called the Typhoon II, it was progressively changed until it had become obvious that it would be a new airplane. The wings of the Tempest I were elliptical in shape, much like the Spitfire's, and used a considerably thinner airfoil, and a later model Napier Sabre IV engine which was rated at 2,240hp and which produced a top speed of 466mph at 25,000ft. It was one of the fastest piston-engined RAF airplanes.

Plans for quantity production of the Mk.I ended when Napier decided not to proceed with the troublesome Sabre IV, which powered only an experimental Tempest II. The production Mk.II used the increasingly reliable 18-cylinder, two-row 2,500hp radial Bristol Centaurus sleeve-valve engine in a longer fuselage with a larger vertical tail.

The Mk.V actually preceded the Mk.II into production and was the only version of the Tempest to see action. It was more like the Mk.I, having a Sabre engine, rated at 2,200hp. In the latter stages of the war, Tempest Mk.Vs led the way in shooting down

Surviving Examples

F Mk.II
RAF MW401 – Brooklands
RAF LA607 – Fantasy of Flight
RAF MW848 – Indian Air Force Museum
RAF MN235 – RAF Museum (Hendon)

TT Mk.V
RAF NV778 – RAF Museum (Hendon)
RAF EJ693 – Fantasy of Flight

the Germans' pilot-less 400mph V-1 'buzz-bombs', which were being launched by the hundreds against London and other heavily populated areas.

Specifications of the Tempest F Mk.II

Length: 34ft 5in
Wingspan: 41ft 0in
Height: 15ft 6in
Wing area: 304 sq ft
Empty weight: 9,300lb
Maximum speed: 440mph at 15,900ft
Maximum range: 1,700 miles
Service ceiling: 37,000ft
Rate of climb: 4,520ft/min

Hawker Typhoon

Several Hawker designs were aimed at replacing the Hurricane, and were powered by incompletely proven engines, with the Typhoon being the only one to achieve true quantity production. It had persistent handling and engine problems that were eventually overcome sufficiently to enable it to achieve recognition as a major type in the latter part of the war in Europe.

The first prototype Typhoon Mk.IA flew in February 1940, revealing a variety of mechanical and design problems. These, plus the need for Hawker to concentrate on Hurricane production, almost led to the Typhoon being cancelled. Production was finally ordered from Gloster in October 1940, with its first airplane, a Mk.IA, flying in May 1941, armed with twelve .30 cal. machine guns. The subsequent Mk.IB carried four 20mm cannon instead.

The engine for the first Typhoon Is was the Napier Sabre I, rated at 2,100hp from 24 cylinders arranged in an 'H' configuration, and displacing 2,238 cu. in. (36.7 liters). It, too, had problems and had been placed in production before all of them had been eliminated.

Initial squadron operations were notable for the high failure rate of the Typhoon airframe, mainly in the tail, and usually blamed on fatigue. Despite this, its high speed at low altitude enabled its pilots to meet the sporadic nuisance raids by Focke Wulf FW 190s on fairly even terms. As more and more operational experience was acquired, many of the problems were solved and the type was being flown by no fewer than 26 RAF squadrons as D-Day approached. It was only when the airplane's superior low-altitude performance was put to use in the ground-support role, with up to 2,000lb of bombs, that it finally demonstrated its greatest usefulness.

Immediately prior to the invasion, Typhoons were used to destroy a series of vital German defensive radar facilities along the French coast, which greatly eased the way for Allied control of the skies over the Normandy beaches.

As Allied forces began to break out of Normandy, and the Germans were forced to fall back, the rocket-equipped Typhoons, in concert with heavily armed USAAF Thunderbolts, became the scourge of German armored units. In the battle of the Falaise Gap, thousands of German tanks, armored cars and other vehicles were reduced to wreckage, making major counter-attacks impossible.

When production of all models of the Typhoon was concluded in 1944, more than 3,300 had been built. It was followed on the production line by the Hawker Tempest V.

Specifications of the Typhoon Mk.IB

Length: 31ft 10in
Wingspan: 41ft 7in
Height: 16ft 4in
Wing area: 279 sq ft
Empty weight: 8,800lb
Maximum speed: 405mph at 18,000ft
Maximum range: 1,000 miles
Service ceiling: 34,000ft
Rate of climb: 3,000 ft/min

Surviving Example

Mk.IB
RAF MN235 – RAF Museum-Hendon (ex-NASM)

Vickers Supermarine Spitfire

Certainly the most famous fighter of World War Two, the Spitfire was not merely an outstanding military airplane, but the symbol of Great Britain's determination to defeat the previously unstoppable German Luftwaffe.

The lineage of the Spitfire guaranteed that it would carry on the record of Supermarine as a producer of exceptional flying machines. The series of Schneider Cup racers that set the world standard for power and speed culminated in R J Mitchell's superlative S.6b. It not only won for Britain permanent possession of one of aviation's premier awards, but in 1931 became the first man-made vehicle to exceed 400mph.

The Spitfire was designed by Mitchell in response to the Air Ministry's 1934 specification for a fighter with a closed cockpit, retractable landing gear and eight machine guns, a very advanced combination for the day. The prototype Mk.I flew in March 1936, and achieved 350mph with its 1,000hp Rolls-Royce Merlin V-12 engine. As evidence of the conflicted thinking within the RAF, nine months later, the first production Hawker Fury II open-cockpit biplane was on its way to becoming a standard RAF fighter, with its 640hp engine good for just 225mph.

On 14 May 1938, the first production Spitfire I flew with a two-bladed, wooden, fixed-pitch propeller, soon to be replaced by a two-position, three-bladed unit, but still with blades of wood The first delivery of a Mk.I came on August 4 at Duxford, and by the start of the war, nine squadrons were equipped with this sleek fighter.

When the Battle of Britain began in the late summer of 1940, another 10 squadrons were ready. With 32 squadrons of Hawker Hurricanes, they bore the brunt of the Battle, with Spitfires usually taking on Messerschmitt Bf 109s, and the somewhat slower

Hurricanes often dealing with the German Heinkel He 111 and Junkers Ju 87 and Ju 88 bombers. Together, they dealt the Luftwaffe its first major defeat. Even more importantly, they forced Hitler to cancel his plans to invade England, then in an advanced stage of preparation.

The Spitfire may have gone through more versions and modifications than any other fighter of World War Two, with most using the 1,650 cu. in. Merlin engine, but others with the 2,240 cu. in. Rolls-Royce Griffon, the direct descendant of the 'R' engine which powered the final Schneider Cup racers. Armament consisted of many combinations of .30 cal. machine guns and 20mm cannon. Some had pressurized cockpits for very high altitude interception, while others had clipped wings for very low altitude maneuverability.

Most had slightly bulged canopies faired into the turtledeck, while the later versions had bubble canopies for improved

visibility. To meet Royal Navy needs, more than 1,200 navalized Seafires were built, complete with arrestor hooks and strengthened landing gears for operation aboard carriers. The Spitfire was even equipped with twin floats, like its racing ancestors, but this variant never got into production.

The story of the Spitfire has become one of aviation's legends, thanks to its superb flying qualities, the artistic shape of its elliptical wing, and its continuing schedule of air show demonstrations by many of the dozens that have survived more than 60 years.

Specifications of the Spitfire Mk.Vc

Length: 29ft 11in
Wingspan: 40ft 2in
Height: 11ft 5in
Wing area: 249 sq ft
Empty weight: 5,100lb
Maximum speed: 374mph at 13,000ft
Maximum range: 1,135 miles
Service ceiling: 37,000ft
Rate of climb:

Surviving Examples

F Mk.Ia
RAF X4590 – RAF Museum (Hendon)
RAF K9942 – RAF Museum (Cosford)
RAF P9306 – Museum of Science and Industry
RAF P9444 – Science Museum (London)
RAF R6915 – Imperial War Museum (London)

F Mk.IIa
RAF P7350 – Battle of Britain Memorial Flight
RAAF P7973 – Australian War Memorial

F Mk.IIb
RAF P8332 – Canadian National Air Museum

F Mk.Vb
RAF AB910 – Battle of Britain Memorial Flight
RAF BL370 – D-Day Museum (New Orleans)
RAF BL614 – RAF Museum (Hendon)

LF Mk.Vb
RAF EP120 – The Fighter Collection
RAF AB910 – Battle of Britain Memorial Flight

F Mk.Vc
RAF AR614 – Flying Heritage Collection
RAF BR545 – RAAF Museum
RAF MA863 – National Museum of the US Air Force

LF Mk.Vc
RAF AR501 – Old Warden Aerodrome
RAF JG891 – Historic Flying, Ltd.

LF Mk.Ve
RAF AB910 – Battle of Britain Memorial Flight

HF Mk.Vc
RAF MA298 – Stauning, Denmark

F Mk.VIIc
RAF EN474 – US National Air & Space Museum

F. Mk.VIII
RAF JF294 – South African National Museum of Military History

F Mk.VIII
RAF NH631– Indian Air Force Historic Flight
RAF MT719 – Cavanaugh Flight Museum

HF Mk.VIIIc
RAF MV154 – Air Museum, North Weald
RAF MV239 – Temora Aviation Museum, New South Wales

TR Mk.8
RAF MT818 – Tillamook (Oregon) Naval Air Station

Mk.IX
RAF 'MH424' (MJ271) – Imperial War Museum (Duxford)
RAF MK356 – Battle of Britain Memorial Flight
RAF MJ772 – Boeing Museum of Flight
RAF MK805 – Italian Air Force Museum
c/n SH/CBAF550 – Rangoon, Burma

Mk.IXb
Old Flying Machine Co.

LF Mk.IXc
RAF MJ143 – Military Air Museum (Soesterberg, Netherlands)
RAF MJ783 – Royale Musee de l'Armee, Brussels
RAF MK356 – Battle of Britain Memorial Flight

RAF EN199 – Malta Aviation Museum,
RAF MA793 – Wings of Dreams
RAF NH188 – Canadian National Aviation Museum

HF Mk.IXc
RAF MJ772 – Boeing Museum of Flight

LF Mk.IXe
RAF EN145 – IDFAF Museum
RAF MH350 – Norwegian Armed Forces Museum

HF Mk.IXe
MRAFL407 – Caroline Grace (Duxford)

TR Mk.9c
RAF H-98 (PV202) – Historic Flying Ltd.

PR Mk.X
RAF PA908 – National Museum of the US Air Force

PR Mk.XI
RAF PL965 – North Weald
RAF PL979 – Royal Norwegian Air Force Collection
The Fighter Collection

F Mk.XIVe
RAF RM689 – Rolls-Royce

FR Mk.XIV
RAF 'MV268' (MV293) – The Fighter Collection

FR Mk.XIVe
c/n 6S/6491270 – Royal Army Museum, Brussels
RAF MT847 – Museum of Science & Industry, Manchester
RAF TE476 – Fantasy of Flight
RAF RM201 – Historic Flying Ltd.
RAF SM914 – Royal Thai Museum
RAF TZ138 – Richmond, B.C., Canada

LF Mk.XVI
RAF MV293 – The Fighter Collection
RAF NH904 – Palm Springs Air Museum
RAF SM411 – Muszeum Loctnictwa, Kracow
RAF TE330 – National Museum of the US Air Force

LF Mk.XVIe
RAF RR263 – Musee de l'Air (Paris)
RAF 'TB675' – RAF Museum (Cosford)
RAF TD248 and RW386 – Historical Flight Ltd.
RAF SL974 – San Diego Air & Space Museum
RAF SM411 – National Air Museum, Kracow, Poland
RAF TB863 – Alpine Fighter Collection
RAF TE311 – Battle of Britain Memorial Flight
RAF TE214 – Canadian National Museum
RAF TE462 – National Museum of Flight Scotland
RAF TE476 – Fantasy of Flight

FR Mk.XVIII
RAF SM845 – National War & Resistance Museum

FR Mk.XVIIIe
RAF SM845 – Historic Flying Ltd.
RAF SM845 – Imperial War Museum (Duxford)

RAF SM986 – Indian Air Force Museum
RAF TP276 – Rudy Frasca (Illinois)

PR.XIX
RAF PM627 – Flygvapenmuseum, Sweden
RAF PM630 – Bangkok
RAF PM631, PS915 – Battle of Britain Historic Flight
RAF PS890 – Planes of Fame

F Mk.22
RAF PK355 – Zimbabwe Air Force Museum
RAF PK481 – Aviation Heritage Museum, Perth

Seafire F Mk.XV
FAA PR376 – Defense Force Museum, Yangon Air Base, Rangoon, Burma
FAA PR451 – Naval Museum of Alberta

Seafire F.17
FAA SX137 – Fleet Air Arm Museum

Chapter Four

Australia

Commonwealth CA-12 Boomerang

When the Royal Australian Air Force (RAAF) faced the oncoming Japanese military offensive in 1941, it was equipped with obsolescent Brewster Buffaloes. It was greatly in need of a new airplane, and went to the brand new Commonwealth Aircraft Co., which promptly turned to one of America's newest airplane manufacturers, the North American Aviation Co. What could have been a recipe for disaster, worked out very well for all concerned.

As war approached in the Far East, the RAAF was informed that its two major suppliers of military airplanes – Great Britain and the USA – could barely fulfill their own domestic needs, and were being forced to cut off deliveries to most other countries. Left to their own devices, the Australians converted one of their most recent trainer acquisitions into a combat airplane that served them well.

North American Aviation had been developing a series of trainers and combination trainers/ground-support airplanes into

barely enough business to remain afloat. They had sold a couple of dozen of these small planes to a variety of countries, some of which did their own modifications in the field to make them into offensive weapons. Two of these NA-16 trainers were sold to the RAAF.

With changes, the NA-16 became the Wirraway, with the fighter version having two .30 cal. machine guns and the dive bomber version able to carry up to 500lb of bombs. It was powered by a 600hp Pratt & Whitney engine (the same that would power many thousands of AT-6 trainers). Despite performance well below that of contemporary Japanese fighters, they played a major role in the defense of Rabaul.

When it came time to create the first Australian fighter, Commonwealth, which had been producing NA-33 trainers (known as the Wackett) on license, decided to modify the design into a much more capable combat machine. The new airplane used the Wackett's wing, tail, landing gear and center fuselage. The engine was a 1,200hp P&W R-1830 Twin Wasp, giving a top speed of almost 300mph with four .30 cal. machine guns and two 20mm cannon.

In tests, the Boomerang out-maneuvered both the American P-39 Airacobra and P-40 Kittyhawk, though both of those had a considerable speed advantage. Surprisingly, the Boomerang could out-climb them at almost 3,000ft/min.

They first went into action in April 1943, and continued to provide defensive cover for Allied operations in the New Guinea area. Australian pilots quickly learned how to make the most of the strengths of the Boomerang and work around its weaknesses.

Other Boomerang-equipped units provided protection for submarine bases in Western Australia into 1945 and over the open seas for convoys. Gradually, however, the slow Boomerangs were replaced by much more capable British and American fighters, though they continued to fly ground-support missions. While not one of the 250 Boomerangs built can be credited for shooting down a single Japanese airplane, it was nevertheless an impressive achievement for a firm that had so little manufacturing experience and even less in designing combat airplanes.

Specifications of the CA-12

Length: 25ft 6in
Wingspan: 36ft 3in
Height: 9ft 7in
Wing area: 225 sq ft
Empty weight: 5,450lb
Maximum speed: 296mph at 7,000ft
Maximum range: 930 miles at 190mph at 15,000ft
Service ceiling: 29,000ft
Rate of climb: 2,900 ft/min

Surviving Example

Boomerang
RAAF A460206 – Royal Australian Aviation Museum

Chapter Five

France

Caudron C.714

The sleek lines of its racing ancestors are hard to miss. From its long nose to its low-set canopy, the Caudron C.714 bears the hallmarks of a line of airplanes that won multiple *Coupes Deutsch* and one Thompson Trophy Race in the mid-1930s. Its engine, while clearly sufficient for closed-course racing, was entirely too low-powered to produce the speed and rate of climb demanded by aerial combat. Few of the 90 that were built got into action, and then only briefly.

Its origins date back to the 1933 *Coupe Deutsch* and include some of the most efficient airplanes ever created. It was the need to add military equipment – guns, ammunition, armor, radios, increased fuel, etc. – that increased the weight, drag, and wing-loading and thus reduced its performance to a level far below that of the Messerschmitt Bf 109.

Nevertheless, it was the only true lightweight fighter to take part in the war, even though most other countries attempted to produce their own. Its empty weight of 3,100lb was 1,500lb below that of the Dewoitine D.520, and 1,100lb below that of the Morane 406, though it had only a 450hp Renault V-12, in contrast to the 910hp Hispano-Suiza V-12 of the other two.

Armament, too, was below even the less-than-ideal French contemporary practice. The Caudron had four .30 cal. machine guns while the Dewoitine had those plus a single 20mm cannon, and the Morane had two machine guns and a 20mm cannon. The

Bf 109E could hit 350mph and carried two .30 cal. machine guns and two 20mm cannon.

The immediate predecessor of the C.714 was the C.710 fighter prototype, which flew in 1936 with fixed landing gear. The C.711 was to have been another racer, but was not built. The C.712R was designed to attack the World Speed Record, and is now confusingly called the C.714R and is on display in the Musee de l'Air, north of Paris. Next came the C.713 Cyclone fighter, which was a C.710 with

retractable landing gear. And finally, the prototype C.714, which flew in the summer of 1938.

After passing the Government tests, the C.714 was awarded a production contract for 100 airplanes, even though it was known to have inferior performance. Such was France's desperate need for airplanes in light of the coming war. Finally facing reality, production was ended, but only after the first 90 were built. Fifty of them were sent to an even more desperate Finland, struggling to hold back the Germans. Hardly any of them arrived at their destination. Others equipped a Polish squadron in the French Air Force and saw limited action in 1940 before France capitulated.

Planned successors to the C.714 began with the Caudron–Renault C.R.760, which reached 350mph in tests on the 730hp of an Isotta Fraschini V-12, but the test airplanes had to be destroyed before the Germans could capture them. The next, a C.R.770 prototype, had an 800hp Renault V-16 and was expected to top out at 365mph, but was badly damaged on its first and only flight in May 1940, and it, too, was scuttled. The final development, the Caudron C.R.780, was to have had a 500hp Renault V-12, along with the impressive armament of two 20mm cannon and either two or four .30 cal. machine guns. It was not built. From that point on, Caudron moved in a completely different direction.

Specifications of the C.714

Length: 32ft 6in
Wingspan: 28ft 6in
Height: 9ft 7in
Wing area: 135 sq ft
Empty weight: 3,835lb
Maximum speed: 367mph at 14,750ft

Maximum range: 930 miles
Service ceiling: 34,000ft
Rate of climb: 2,400ft/min

Surviving Example

C.714

c/n CA556 – Central Air Museum of Finland

Morane Saulnier M.S. 406

The M.S.406 could easily be considered a symbol of so much that went wrong with French military policy in the run-up to World War Two. It was acquired in greater numbers than any other type of fighter prior to the fall of France, even though it was a 1935 design that was obsolete before the first one reached its operational unit. The pursuit squadrons equipped with them were at a predictable disadvantage when they met Messerschmitt 109s and even Ju 88s in the skies above France.

The first prototype of what was originally called the M.S.405 made its initial flight in August 1935. With its 860hp Hispano-Suiza V-12 engine it could reach 250mph at sea level and almost 300mph at 13,000ft. At that stage, its performance was roughly equal to that of the prototype Bf 109s. Development progressed slowly, however, with official tests not completed until mid-1937, by which time the first Messerschmitt Bf 109s were in squadron service. Production of the M.S.406 began in June 1938, when 109s had already been tested in combat for several months in the Spanish Civil War.

At the start of World War Two more than 500 airplanes had been sent to units of the French Air Force, and some 1,000 had been delivered by the time France surrendered. And while the French

Specifications of the M.S.406

Length: 26ft 9in
Wingspan: 34ft 10in
Height: 9ft 4in
Wing area: 172 sq ft
Empty weight: 4,190lb
Maximum speed: 302mph at 16,400ft
Maximum range: 500 miles
Service ceiling: 30,850ft
Rate of climb: 3,550ft/min

Surviving Example

M.S.406
Musee de l'Air (Paris)

put up a valiant fight, the airplane was simply out of date, and almost half were destroyed in the air or on the ground.

Other countries made considerable use of the M.S.406, or at least tried. Poland ordered 160, of which 50 had been sent but not received by the time Poland fell. The rest were then sent on to China, but ended up in the hands of French colonial forces in Indonesia. Thirty were sold to Finland, which added more than 50 captured by the Germans in France and used them against the Soviets. The latter were soon re-equipped with captured Russian 1,100hp engines, which produced a major improvement in their performance.

France continued to build Moranes in the unoccupied portion of the country, and some were operated by the Vichy government in the Middle East. A few others were converted into M.S.410s with major wing modifications, and flown by the Croatians.

Overall, the out-dated and underpowered M.S.406 provided good target practice for its enemies.

Dewoitine D.520

This was the fighter the French Air Force (Armee de l'Air) needed when the war started in September 1939. It had the performance and the armament to cope with German Air Force (Luftwaffe) attackers. But it was several years of development behind the ineffective Morane-Saulnier 460.

It was a direct descendant of the Dewoitine D.500 series, though any similarities were difficult to spot. The 520 used the ubiquitous Huispano-Suiza 12Y series of V-12 engines, in its case a version rated at 900hp driving a two-bladed, fixed-pitch wooden propeller. With this combination, the prototype could reach 325mph at 20,000 and climb to 13,000ft in four minutes.

A government order for 200 airplanes was placed as soon as the official trials were completed in March 1939. Four hundred more were ordered in June as war clouds darkened, but the first production airplane did not fly until December, when the war had been in progress for several months. In June 1940, when the German Army invaded France, 100 520s were being built per month, though only one active unit of the Armee de l'Air was flying them at this time.

In the short period between the German invasion and the surrender of most of France, four Dewoitine-equipped units claimed more than 100 victories over the Germans, who previously had faced no meaningful aerial opposition. Most of the French fighters were then ferried to North Africa, to join others already there. Meanwhile, the factory proceeded with unrealistic, if not purely imaginary plans to place the improved D.521 into production with a 1,000hp Rolls-Royce Merlin engine. Only a prototype was tested before the Germans marched in.

On 25 June 1940, the war ended for the nation of France, but the southeast portion of the country remained unoccupied, though it was governed from Vichy and generally collaborated with the Nazis. The D.520 was being produced for the Vichy Air Force, which eventually had nine fighter groups in operation. Dewoitines were operated against the British at Gibraltar. When the Germans

took over the remainder of France in late 1942, they seized a large quantity of flyable Dewoitines, some of which they used to train fighter pilots.

Others were transferred to captive air forces in Rumania and Bulgaria, which used them operationally. Sixty went to the Italian Air Force (Reggia Aeronautica) as trainers. Limited production continued under German ownership, which tested an advanced version, the 520Z, the single example of which carried three 20mm cannon and had a 1,600hp Hispano engine that drove it to more than 400mph.

When the Germans were finally driven out of southern France, a group of loyal French Air Force pilots grabbed D.520s, attacking the retreating German Army units. Including 180 D.520s built after the armistice, total production was about 610 airplanes.

Specifications of the D.520

Length: 28ft 9in
Wingspan: 33ft 6in
Height: 8ft 5in
Wing area: 172 sq ft
Empty weight: 4,610lb
Maximum speed: 329mph at 19,700ft
Maximum range: 775 miles
Service ceiling: 36,100ft
Rate of climb: 2,360ft/min

Surviving Example

D.520
c/n 603 or 862 – Musee de l'Air (Paris)

Chapter Six
Czechoslovakia

Avia B.534

The early 1930s were the heyday of the biplane fighter, with its nostalgic multitude of struts and wires, its open cockpit and its non-retractable landing gear, each creating its special wind noises. While monoplane fighters had been known as far back as World War One, and the value of streamlining had been established by a series of French Deperdussin racers as early as 1913, there remained strong resistance to single-winged pursuits owing to continued fears of structural weakness.

One of the best and last of these traditional forms was the Avia B.534, built in Czechoslovakia, which, itself, was a creation of that 'War to end all wars'. The B.534 was the ultimate development of the B.34, built in Prague in 1932 for the Czech Army Air Force. It went through improvements: B.134, B.234, B.334, B.434 and finally to the 534, which had a 750hp Hispano-Suiza 12Y. It had a top speed of 227mph, which was quite respectable at the time.

The Czechs entered several 534s in the 1937 International Flying Competition at Zurich, Switzerland, where it was a serious challenger to the early Bf 109 in several events. The B.534-III and -IV had engines that produced 100hp more than the first Avia-built Hisso engine, and had a closed canopy, which combined to boost the top speed to 245mph.

At the time of the Munich Crisis of September 1938, Czech Air Force units had more than 300 534s, but before they could be used against the Germans, the latter had occupied their country without organized resistance.

The Czech airplanes were taken over by the Luftwaffe which, sufficiently impressed, equipped a pursuit unit with them, though only briefly. The Germans then used them primarily as trainers and glider tugs. Three squadrons were formed in the newly-created, German-controlled Slovak Air Force and were sent to the Russian front in mid-1941. They fought the Red Air Force in the Ukraine, but were out-performed by the enemy's MiGs and Yaks, and were returned to non-combat duty.

A follow-on design was planned by the Czech government while it remained in power, and could have proven significant. The Avia Av.135 was a low-wing monoplane with retractable landing gear and a 900hp Avia 12Y V-12. It could top 330mph and climb at more than 2,500ft/min. An improved version – the Av-35-3 – was ordered by the Bulgarian Air Force. Twelve were delivered, but that was the end of the Avia works' independent operations until the war ended.

Specifications of the B.534

Length: 26ft 11in
Wingspan: 33ft 10in
Height: 9ft 2in
Wing area: 254 sq ft
Empty weight: 3,220lb
Maximum speed: 245mph at 14,450ft
Maximum range: 360 miles
Service ceiling: 34,875ft
Rate of climb: 2,950ft/min

Surviving Example

B.534
Prague-Kbely, Czech Republic

Chapter Seven

Union of Soviet Socialist Republics

Lavochkin La-7

The story of the La-7 begins with the LAGG-1, which was developed for the 1938 competition to create a modern fighter for the then-antiquated Red Air Force. The I-22 prototype flew in March 1939, powered by an 1,100hp M-105P V-12 engine which gave it a top speed of 375mph at altitude, even though the aircraft was overweight and had insufficiently effective controls. With some changes, it went into production in 1940. When, early in 1941, the engine was changed, it was called the LaGG-3.

Like the original, the -3 was built almost entirely of readily available wood, with only the control surfaces being metal. It had greater range and could carry a wide variety of machine guns and cannon. By 1942, there were more LaGG-3s in service than any other type.

In mid-1942, the -3 was replaced by the La-5 which had the same basic airframe, but a 1,700hp Shvetsov 14-cylinder radial engine, and thus a very different profile. It was initially flown in late 1941 and soon displayed speed and maneuverability at low altitude superior to the latest Bf 109F. While the first La-5s off the assembly line were modified LaGG-3s, they were replaced by the new design which included a semi-bubble canopy for improved pilot vision.

The La-5 went into mass production in late May 1942 and saw its first action during the epic battle of Stalingrad. Gradually, the wood construction was replaced by metal and the weight reduced, at the same time as a more powerful engine was introduced. While it still trailed other countries' first-line fighters in many respects, it served the purposes for which it was designed, being sturdy and easy to repair by quickly trained ground crews.

Development continued, with the La-7 appearing in 1943. The once-insufficient armament had grown to three 20mm cannon, while the long-standard load of rockets and/or several hundred pounds of bombs was retained. In order to boost the speed or shorten the take-off roll under difficult conditions, a liquid-fuel rocket motor was located in the rear fuselage. It reportedly increased the maximum speed from 415mph to 450–475mph for short bursts.

Specifications of the La-7

Length: 27ft 11in
Wingspan: 32ft 2in
Height: 9ft 3in
Wing area: 189 sq ft
Loaded weight: 7,495lb
Maximum speed: 430mph at 16,400ft
Maximum range: 395 miles
Service ceiling: 33,300ft
Rate of climb: 4:30 to 16,400ft

La-7
Russian Air Force Museum
Czech '77' – Praha-Kbely, Prague (Czech-built S.97)

Lavochkin La-9

The final World War Two version in the series was the La-9, a cleaned-up La-7 that was built almost entirely of metal and had an 1,870hp version of the Shvetsov radial engine. This produced a top speed at sea level of 428mph, increased rate of climb, and higher service ceiling. It was equipped with three and then four 20mm cannon. Test versions used a variety of techniques to boost speed, including twin rocket motors mounted under the wings, or two ram-jet engines, or even two pulse-jets like those that powered German V-1 buzz-bombs.

Deliveries began in 1945, with the result that few La-9s saw action. Yet another version – the La-11 – was built after the war and equipped squadrons until the first of the jets became available.

Specifications of the La-9

Length: 30ft 2in
Wingspan: 34ft 9in
Height: 9ft 8in
Wing area: 189 sq ft
Empty weight: 5,775 lb
Maximum speed: 428mph at sea level
Maximum range: 615 miles
Service ceiling: 36,500ft
Rate of climb: 3,840ft/min

La-9
Imperial War Museum (Duxford)

Mikoyan and Gurevich MiG-3

The urgency with which modernization was pressed was evident in the Soviet aircraft industry's achievements, especially in the MiG series. Created by future stars of the early jet age, Artem Mikoyan and Mikhail Gurevich, the MiG-1 looked very much like an airplane that could hold its own with Messerschmitts and Spitfires. It moved from drawing board to first test flight in four months, and then to combat in less than a year, suggesting that some stages in the development process may have been too rushed.

With a 1,350hp Mikulin liquid-cooled V-12 it could reach nearly 400mph at altitude, and climb almost to 40,000ft. Due to shortages of aluminum alloys, the outer panels of the wings and the rear fuselage and tail were built from heavier wood. Armament was limited to a single .50 cal. and a pair of .30 cal. machine guns. It retained the pilot-preferred open cockpit of earlier airplanes.

While it was unquestionably superior to the Polikarpov fighters it replaced, its value in combat was limited by poor stability, even once a pilot learned to deal with its poor low-speed handling characteristics. It was then replaced on the assembly line by the MiG-3 after just a few months. Aviation's old saying that 'if an airplane looks right, it will fly right' did not apply in this instance.

The MiG-3 offered greater armament (two .30 cal. and three .50 cal. machine guns), greater range (an additional internal tank) and improved stability thanks to dihedral of the outer wing panels. All these changes made it a better airplane, but its inferior

Specification of the MiG-3

Length: 26ft 9in
Wingspan: 33ft 10in
Height: 8ft 7in
Wing area: 189 sq ft
Loaded weight: 7,385lb
Maximum speed: 398mph at 25,590ft
Maximum range: 776 miles at 342mph
Service ceiling: 39,370ft
Rate of climb: 5:42 to 16,400ft

Surviving Examples

MiG-3
The Fighter Factory
Novosibirsk, Russia

maneuverability posed a serious problem once it met the enemy in dogfights.

The production of the MiG-1 and MiG-3 was brief, once the supply of Mikulin engines was absorbed by much-needed Ilyushin Il-2 Sturmovik anti-tank airplanes. The highly-modified MiG-5, which was a -3 with a 1,600hp radial engine, ended up slower than the earlier airplane. The armament of the final -5s was reduced to just four .30 cal. machine guns. It could hardly have been satisfactory, as only a few MiG-5s got into combat in 1943. Future efforts by the design team would be directed towards fighters powered by turbojet engines, none of which were built during World War Two.

Polikarpov I-15

The I-15 Chaika (Gull) was a particularly clean biplane. With a 700hp M-25V radial engine (license-built Wright R-1820 Cyclone), it could reach 225mph and climb to 33,000ft. When it arrived during October 1933, it was one of the fastest fighters in the world, though few people outside the secretive USSR had any idea that Soviet technology was in any position to challenge the West.

Known initially as the TsKB-3, it had a gull-shaped top wing to give its pilots a better forward view than with a strut-mounted wing. It carried four .30 cal. machine guns, which was more than most fighters of its day. In late 1935, a modified I-15 was flown by Viktor Kokkinaki to a world altitude record of almost 48,000ft. Its first taste of combat came during the Spanish Civil War, when more than 500 I-15s and improved I-15bis were operated by the Republican forces. When up against even the earliest of Luftwaffe Bf 109s. they may have had superior maneuverability, but lacked the all-out speed needed in the evolving modern version of aerial battles.

In late 1939 when the Red Army invaded neighboring Finland, it counted among its air force types the I-15, many of them operating off the snow on skis. Later, when Germany attacked the USSR, its Messerschmitts and Junkers ran into increasingly obsolete Polikarpov biplanes which were soon withdrawn, having been proven ineffective.

An improved I-15, called the I-15bis, had its top wing mounted more conventionally on cabane struts, and a slightly more powerful M-25 engine inside a more streamlined cowl. It was used extensively in the Spanish Civil War as well as against Finland in the early stages of World War Two. Some of those were captured by the Finns and added to their limited air force. The I-15bis, one of the first fighters to carry air-to-ground rockets, remained in service with first-line units of the Red Air Force until late in 1941, having by then been completely outclassed by the Luftwaffe.

The I-15 series was far from an operational success, but it provided valuable experience for all phases of military flying. The Soviet aircraft industry was still struggling to catch up with those of the major air powers.

Specifications of the I-15

Length: 20ft 8in
Wingspan: 30ft 0in
Height: 9ft 7in
Wing area: 225 sq ft
Empty weight: 2,595lb
Maximum speed: 224mph
Maximum range: 450 miles
Service ceiling: 32,800ft
Rate of climb: 2,500 ft/min

Surviving Examples

I-15
m/s 02089 – Imperial War Museum (Duxford)
The Fighter Factory

Polikarpov I-16

In the early 1930s it was becoming clear that the days of the biplane fighter were numbered and that only low-wing monoplanes could achieve the significant increases in speed needed to gain aerial supremacy. What wasn't so clear was which country would lead the way, nor just how pilot concerns over high landing speeds and the presumed weaknesses of internally-braced wings would be dealt with.

The USSR, unlike other nations, proceeded to develop modern retractable landing gear monoplanes in parallel with biplanes having traditional fixed landing gear. Both styles had strong support among pilots and designers, with some preferring the monoplane's greater speed and payload and others favoring the biplane's superior maneuverability. Hence, the I-16 prototype first flew within a few weeks of the I-15 and joined it in action in Spain and later on the Eastern Front.

The prototype I-16 first flew in February 1934, and on only its second flight, was clocked at 282mph. making it the fastest fighter design in the world. But with speed came extended take-off and landing runs, necessitating the enlargement of most Red Air Force airfields, which were crude by world standards, and delaying the start of production of the type until late 1935. Flying what was then a 'high-performance' airplane brought problems for the pilots, who were used to docile biplanes that took off and landed slowly. Questionable stability, in particular, was to plague the I-16 throughout its service life.

The I-16 Type 4 had a 730hp M-25A (Wright Cyclone) engine, good for 283mph at 10,000ft and a maximum cruising range of 510 miles. Armament consisted of a pair of .30 cal. machine guns, less than the standard for the time. Soon after the start of the Spanish Civil War in July 1938, I-16s were shipped to Spain, ultimately equipping seven squadrons of 15 fighters each. In action, Soviet pilots were able to out-fly the German Heinkel He 51, but not the Italian Fiat CR.32. It became an expensive way to learn some important lessons.

This led to the Type 10, with four .30 cal. machine guns and the slightly more powerful M-25V engine. Arriving in Spain in late 1937, they were the first to meet pilots flying the Messerschmitt Bf 109B, and proved its equal, though not its superior. More than 475 I-16s found their way to Spain, along with their Soviet pilots, crews and support personnel. Eventually the men were evacuated, and replaced by Soviet-trained Spaniards.

Additional Type 10s were built in Spain, some of them after the end of the Civil War, in March 1939, and served with the Spanish Air Force. Since that air arm never flew in combat, much about the airplanes' actual usefulness remains a mystery.

Specifications of the I-16, Type 24

Length: 20ft 1in
Wingspan: 29ft 7in
Height: 8ft 5in
Wing area: 161 sq ft
Empty weight: 3,285lb
Maximum speed: 326mph at sea level
Maximum range: 435 miles with two 26-gallon auxiliary tanks
Service ceiling: 29,350ft
Rate of climb: 2,800 ft/min

Surviving Examples

I-16
The Fighter Factory
USSR 2421014 – Flying Heritage Collection

Polikarpov I-153

The final development of the I-15 was the I-153, which was a rarity among biplane fighters, in that it had retractable landing gear, but reverted to the gull-style top wing of its I-15 predecessor. With a 1,100hp Shvetsov M-63 (license-built Wright Cyclone) 9-cylinder radial engine, it could reach 267mph at 16,400ft, making it the fastest biplane fighter ever in quantity production. It was developed primarily to counter the Japanese Mitsubishi A5M 'Claude', in the Russo–Japanese conflict.

The prototype first flew in 1938, powered by a 750hp M-25 engine, while the production versions which were built starting in 1939, used the larger power plant. Like most biplane fighters it had an open cockpit, still much preferred by many pilots who were convinced they needed to feel the wind in order to fly their best. Its normal range of 298 miles at cruising speed was stretched to 560 miles when carrying a pair of 26-gallon auxiliary fuel tanks slung under the wings.

Construction of the fuselage combined a wood and steel skeleton with covering of sheet metal from the cockpit forward, and fabric aft.

The wings were wood-covered with fabric. Armament consisted of four .30 cal. machine guns and, when used in the ground-support role, either six air-to-ground rockets or two 165lb bombs.

I-153s were used in quantity by the Soviets against Finland, as well in the Far East and, along with its immediate predecessors, against the Germans on the Eastern Front. It remained in service until 1942, thus becoming one of the last biplane fighters of any air force to be retired in favor of monoplanes.

Specifications of the I-153

Length: 20ft 3in
Wingspan: 32ft 10in
Height: 9ft 3in
Wing area: 238 sq ft
Empty weight: 3,170lb
Maximum speed: 267mph at 16,400ft
Maximum range: 560 miles at 174mph with two 26-gallon auxiliary tanks
Service ceiling: 35,145ft
Rate of climb: 3,300 ft/min

Surviving Examples

I-153
Musee de l'Air (Paris)
The Fighter Factory
Wanaka

Yakovlev Yak-1

Until the modern Yakovlev fighters appeared in the summer of 1941, Red Air Force fighter squadrons were equipped primarily with various versions of Polikarpov I-15 and I-16, using technology dating back to the mid-1930s. With a major air war obviously in the offing, the Soviets knew they had to modernize their equipment quickly.

But they weren't in a position to do what was necessary. There was a serious shortage of aluminum alloy, and of the kind of machinery and skilled machinists required to make the best use of it. They had no engine comparable in power and weight to the German DB600-series. And by the time production had begun in earnest, German troops were deep into the USSR and factories had to be picked up in their entirety and moved many hundreds of miles to the east, where they were safer from bombing attacks.

A competition for fighter designs was won by future star Alexander Yakovlev, whose previous work had concentrated on training and sport airplanes. His I-26, which bore more than a slight resemblance to the Hawker Hurricane, flew in prototype form in March 1939. It out-performed its main rival, the I-22 (which became the LaGG-1) by a considerable margin and was immediately scheduled for mass production, there being no time to waste.

The first I-26s (known as the Yak-1) entered service in 1941, even though they were seriously outclassed in most respects by Luftwaffe Bf 109s and FW 190s. It was only at low altitude that the heavy, mostly-wood, Yak-1 could hold its own. It was powered by an 1,100hp Klimov M-105PA inverted V-12 developed from the French Hispano-Suiza 12Y and turning a three-bladed metal propeller. Armament included two .30 cal. machine guns, a single 20mm cannon firing through the propeller hub, and six 25lb air-to-ground unguided rockets.

But it remained a very basic airplane, with no gyro instruments, an antiquated gun sight and a simple, single-channel radio. In part due to the simplicity of its structure and lack of sophisticated equipment, the Yak-1 could be turned out in large numbers by a rapidly assembled workforce learning its trade on the job.

Greater horsepower increased the level speed, but steady weight increases reduced the rate of climb. Continued improvements, based on experience in the field, led to the Yak-1 being replaced on the production lines by the very similar Yak-7A.

Specifications of the Yak-1

Length: 27ft 10in
Wingspan: 32ft 10in
Height: 8ft 8in
Wing area: 185 sq ft
Empty weight: 5,135lb

Maximum speed: 364mph at 16,400ft
Maximum range: 435 miles at 323mph
Service ceiling: 32,800ft
Rate of climb: 4:30 to 16,400ft

Surviving Example

Yak-1
Hawker Restorations

Yakovlev Yak-3

In 1942, experiments were begun with a Yak-1M aimed at major performance improvements based on the tried-and-true formula of making an airplane cleaner, lighter and more powerful. To this end, the airframe was smoothed and protuberances removed, and the overall size was reduced by cutting the wingspan by 2.5ft and wing area by 25 sq ft. The loaded weight was lowered some 650lb, due in great measure to the increased availability of lightweight aluminum alloys for its basic structure. The power output of the Klimov engine was increased by more than 100hp, with performance increasing accordingly.

One production Yak-3 was tested with the 1,600hp Klimov M-107 engine as used by the Yak-9U, achieving a claimed 447mph. Production of this version was too late to have any impact on the war. Most Yak-3s were used for escort and ground-support operations, though the armament of a single 20mm cannon and two .50 cal. machine guns seems light for the latter purpose.

The Yak-3 first saw action in the summer of 1943 during the battle of Kursk, in which the Red Army's victory led directly to the final defeat of the German land forces. A year later, a group of French volunteer pilots, formed as the Normandie-Niémen Group, fought alongside the Red Air Force in their Yak-3s.

Specifications of the Yak-3

Length: 27ft 11in
Wingspan: 30ft 2in
Height: 7ft 10in
Wing area: 160 sq ft
Loaded weight: 5,865lb
Maximum speed: 403mph at 16,400ft
Maximum range: 560 miles at 193mph
Service ceiling: 35,475ft
Rate of climb: 4:30 to 16,400ft

Surviving Examples

Yak-3
Civil G-BTHD – Imperial War Museum (Duxford)
Planes of Fame
Fighter Factory
m/s unk. – Musee de l'Air (Paris)

Yakovlev Yak-9

The ultimate development of the Yak series of single-seat V-12-powered fighters was the Yak-9, of which considerably more than 15,000 were built, though reliable production records have never been found, assuming they existed in the first place.

The first major production version was the Yak-9D with increased fuel capacity in an effort to improve the unsatisfactory range of the Yak-1 and Yak-7. All had excellent low-altitude maneuverability,

but, with only 1,260hp from a Klimov M-105 V-12 engine, lacked the speed needed to cope with Bf 109s and He 111s, let alone FW 190s and Ju 88s.

Next came the Yak-9DD with even greater fuel capacity required to escort USAAF bombers part of the way on shuttle missions. The Yak-9K used a 45mm cannon to attack heavy armor and light shipping, while the Yak-9T originally used a 37mm cannon, but was tested with several other sizes.

The Yak-9U finally got the more powerful M-107 engine, and had a top speed of 415mph at 16,000ft. The final version – the Yak-9P – had increased navigational and radio equipment, as the Red Air Force gradually upgraded in its efforts to match the utility of fighters of other nations.

In all, some 30,000 Yak fighters of this series were produced, with no authoritative figures on how many of each type were built. In recent years, Yak-3s and Yak-9Us have been built to order in Russia, using original tooling and Allison V-1710 engines supplied by the customer. While highly rugged, they show some signs of crude workmanship, characteristic of their wartime mass production.

Specifications of the Yak-9T

Length: 28ft 1in
Wingspan: 32ft 10in
Height: 8ft 0in
Wing area: 186 sq ft
Empty weight: 6,065lb
Maximum speed: 363mph at 16,400ft
Maximum range: 516 miles at 177mph
Service ceiling: 36,090ft
Rate of climb: 5:23 to 16,400ft

Surviving Examples

Yak-9
Musee de l'Air (Paris)

Chapter Eight

Poland

PZL P.11c

It was considered one of the best of the mid-1930s European fighters, but when thrown into combat against the early Bf 109s, it could call on only its superior maneuverability to save it. However, due to its attractive, almost sporty lines and gull wing, it became an instant hit with aeromodellers.

The Polish fighter began as the P.11a, powered by a 500hp Skoda (license-built Bristol Mercury) radial engine in 1933, 30 being delivered in 1934 with two .30 cal. machine guns. A few were pressed into combat when the war started, but most were used as trainers for later models. The P.11b was the export version using a 595hp Romanian-built Gnome Rhone, as the first batch of 50 was for the Rumanian Air Force.

The P.11c followed in 1935, 1,275 being built for the Polish Air Force with improved pilot visibility and double the number of guns, though most of the production run was armed with only

P.24a, which resembled the P.11c except for its closed cockpit and longer cowling. Evidence of the high regard held for the Polish manufacturer's products was the ordering of more than 100 P.24s by Bulgaria, Greece, Rumania and Turkey, the latter two also acquiring production licenses.

The final version of the P.11 was the P.11g, which had an 840hp Bristol Mercury engine and improved machine guns, but was not ready in time for the start of the brief blitzkrieg war. No Polish fighters are known to have continued in production after the German occupation.

Specifications for the P.11c

Length: 24ft 10in
Wingspan: 35ft 2in
Height: 9ft 4in
Wing area: 193 sq ft
Empty weight: 2,525lb
Maximum speed: 242mph at 18,000ft
Maximum range: 503mph at 155mph
Service ceiling: 36,100ft
Rate of climb: 2,625 ft/min

Surviving Example

P.11c
Polish c/n 562? – National Aviation Museum, Kracow

two. By the time of the German invasion in September 1939, 12 squadrons were active, with 125 P.11cs. Records are lacking, but it is known that several of them got into combat against Ju 87s and other Luftwaffe airplanes. At one time, the sole surviving P.11c was thought to be the actual airplane that shot down the first invading airplane of the war.

The PZL P.24 was the export version of the P.11c and flew for the first time in March 1933. The prototype had a 770hp Gnome Rhone 14-cylinder radial engine, while the version used to demonstrate before potential customers had an upgraded 930hp Gnome-Rhone. Yet another pre-production machine became the

Chapter Nine

The Netherlands

Fokker D.XXI

This is yet another of the mid-1930s European fighters, though with better performance than some. It was designed to meet the announced needs of the Royal Netherlands Indies (now Indonesian) Army, which then changed its mind after the first prototype had flown in March 1936, and ordered none. In 1937, the Dutch Army Air Service stepped in and ordered 36 of them with 830hp Bristol Mercury engines.

The next year, Finland ordered seven fighters, powered by the 830hp version of the Mercury, with intentions to put the design into production. The Spanish Republican government, then involved in a civil war, started licensed production, but the factory was captured before the first fighter could be flown. The next interest came from Denmark, which ordered two airplanes and also set out to build more under license, but only eight had entered service by the time the little country was taken over by Germany.

While slowly building D.XXIs for the Netherlands, Fokker began studying possible improved versions with engines as large as the 925hp Hispano-Suiza 12Y. Even more substantial improvements were envisaged for retractable-landing gear versions powered by the Bristol Hercules, Rolls-Royce Merlin or Daimler-Benz 601. None of these ideas got beyond the discussion stage before the war overtook the Low Countries.

When the German Army invaded the Netherlands, 29 D.XXIs were on the line with three Fighter Groups. And while many of them got into the air and their pilots made valiant efforts to stop the Luftwaffe, they lacked the speed and firepower. After a few days, they had used up all their ammunition and remained grounded when the Germans moved in.

Although the Koolhoven F.K.58 was not a true development of the D.XXI, it was designed by the same engineer and bore a significant physical resemblance. The F.K.58 was a later airplane, the first prototype not flying until September 1938. It was cleaner and had a more powerful 1,080hp Hispano-Suiza 14A radial engine which gave it a top speed of 313mph. Licensed production was to have been in the hands of a Belgian company, but no airplanes had been completed by the time of the German invasion. Of the 18 built in the Netherlands, most went to the French, who equipped several squadrons made up of ex-Polish Air Force pilots who had escaped when their country was overrun.

Specifications for the D.XXI

Length: 26ft 11in
Wingspan: 36ft 1in
Height: 9ft 8in
Wing area: 174 sq ft
Empty weight: 3,200lb
Maximum speed: 286mph
Maximum range: 590 miles at 55% power
Absolute ceiling: 37.900ft
Rate of climb: 1:21 to 16,400ft

Surviving Example

D.XXI
221 – Aviadome, Amsterdam

Fokker G.1

Large, heavy twin-engined fighters were on the minds of many air force planners in the late 1930s, though only the Mosquito and P-38 Lightning fully achieved what they were meant for. Others turned out to be too large and heavy to be maneuverable, and underpowered, though many of them carried impressive armament.

Among the designs was the Fokker G.1, a P-38-like twin which first flew in March 1937, with a pair of 700hp P&W R-1525 Twin Wasp Jr. two-row radial engines. Armed with two 20mm cannon and three .30 cal. machine guns, it could carry up to 880lb of bombs, suggesting it might have been considered a fighter-bomber.

The first to buy the export model was the Spanish Republican government, which needed it for the developing Spanish Civil War.

This G.1a carried a three-man crew including a radio operator and a gunner to man the machine gun in the tail of the central fuselage. Thirty-six were to have gone to Spain, but the Dutch placed an embargo on them, as well as on Estonia, which was suspected of being a front for the Spanish.

When the Netherlands was attacked by Germany in May 1940, two dozen G.1as were flyable, but many were destroyed before they could get into the air. Those that survived the initial raids were thrown into the battle, but their lack of speed and maneuverability resulted in all but one of them being destroyed by the hundreds of German fighters that accompanied their bombers.

Some remained at the Fokker factory and were taken over by the Germans and used as trainers, along with a small order that had been placed by Denmark.

Specifications for the G.1a

Length: 37ft 9in
Wingspan: 56ft 3in
Height: 11ft 2in
Wing area: 412 sq ft
Empty weight: 7,325lb
Maximum speed: 295mph
Maximum range: 945 miles
Service ceiling: 30,500ft
Rate of climb: 2,735 ft/min

Surviving Example

G.1a
330 – Aviadome, Amsterdam

Chapter Ten

Finland

Humu

The airplane on which the Humu was based was built with modern materials, yet was a failure in the service of several air forces. The Humu was re-engineered to be mostly of wood, and so stood little chance of being able to compete against more advanced fighters. Nevertheless, the national airplane manufacturer proceeded to build a prototype, fight test it for almost 20 hours and then decide

it had more than enough major problems to prevent it from going into squadron use.

The earlier design was the Brewster F2A Buffalo, the US Navy's first monoplane fighter. While several hundred were built and most of them delivered to the US Navy, almost 90 found their way to Finland during late 1940 and early 1941. They served the Finns well until the middle of 1944, regardless of the fact that the Red Air Force had long since been equipped with more modern Lavochkin, MiG and Yak fighters.

Despite the increasing obsolescence of the design, the Finns proceeded to build a prototype of what was in effect a wooden Buffalo, flying it in August 1944. Test flights revealed excessive weight, lack of sufficient power and the resultant lack of performance. The sole Humu has been restored and is on display as an example of what a smaller country can do when under extreme pressure.

Specifications

Length: 26ft 4in
Wingspan: 35ft 0in
Height: 12ft 0in
Wing area: 209 sq ft
Maximum weight: 6,380lb

Maximum speed: 267mph estimated
Service ceiling: 26,250ft estimated
Rate of climb: 2,615ft/min estimated

Surviving Example

Humu
Finland 632667 – Central Air Museum of Finland

Pyörremyrsky

In five years of World War Two, Finland fought off the invading USSR in the Winter War, signed a peace treaty, again fought the USSR in the Continuation War as an ally of Germany, and finally accepted the USSR's terms, which included helping chase the Germans out of northern Finland. All through this, it had little domestic aircraft industry and was forced to operate Bf 109s , along with sub-standard American Brewster Buffaloes much of the time.

Only in 1943 did the Finns' *Valtion Lentokonetehdas* begin designing a fighter for the Finnish air force. While it looked a lot like a Bf 109 from the spinner back to the wing (it was powered by a Daimler Benz DB 605 engine), it was an original design, with extensive use of native woods in the wings, tail and fuselage. In contrast, the forward fuselage was built from welded chrome-molybdenum steel and covered with sheet metal panels.

The prototype was completed in late 1944, but as the country was now at peace with its former enemies, there was no need to place it in production. That single example of the 'Whirlwind' has been restored and is on display.

Specifications

Length: 29ft 11in
Wingspan: 34ft 2in
Height: 12ft 9in
Wing area: 205 sq ft
Empty weight: 5,760lb
Maximum speed: 404mph
Maximum range: 2.5 hours with drop tanks
Service ceiling: 37,500ft
Rate of climb: 3,650 ft/min

Surviving Example

Pyörremyrsky
c/n PM1 – Central Air Museum of Finland

Chapter Eleven
Germany

Horten Ho.IX/Go.229V-3

With the Third Reich crumbling around them, Hitler's aeronautical scientists and engineers were still behaving as if the war would last for years, and the very next advanced design would surely turn the tide of battle. One of the most radical designs for any jet fighter was the Horten Ho.IX, a true flying wing with no vertical tail surfaces. It was to have gone into production as the Gotha Go.229.

The Horten brothers had been designing and building increasingly efficient sailplanes for soaring competitions, and continuing to deceive the German Air Ministry into thinking they were developing military airplanes well into the war. Then, based on what they had learned with their sailplanes, they proposed a twin-jet fighter of unusually low drag. The first prototype was flown as a glider in mid-1944, and the second was flown with two 1,900lb. Jumo 004 turbojets. It reached 500mph before being lost in a crash. Much of the airframe was built from a wood/cork laminate, which would have reduced its radar signature in the manner of much later stealth airplanes.

The third prototype (-V3) was ready for test flying and plans were moving ahead for production of 20 fighter-bombers by the Gotha Works when the factory was captured by the US Army and all creative activity ceased. Major portions of the -V3 were shipped to the United States and placed in long-term storage by what eventually became the National Air & Space Museum. Restoration, however, appears to be quite low on the priority list.

Specification of the Ho.IX/Go.229A

Length: 24ft 6in
Wingspan: 55ft 0in
Height: 9ft 2in
Wing area: 40 sq ft
Maximum weight: 18,700lb

Maximum speed: 640mph at 21,000ft estimated
Maximum range: 1,180 miles estimated
Service ceiling: 51,000ft estimated
Rate of climb: 4,300ft/min estimated

Surviving Example

Gotha Go.229V-3
USAAF FE-490 – US National Air & Space Museum

Messerschmitt Bf 109

It is probable that more Messerschmitt 109s were built than any other military airplane, before or since. For much of World War Two, it was the primary fighter of Germany's Luftwaffe, and at various times was the most effective fighter in any air force. The first prototype flew in September 1935, powered by a British Rolls-Royce Kestrel engine, and in defiance of international law that prohibited the building and flying of military airplanes by Germany.

Two production prototypes of the Bf 109B were sent to Spain in late 1936 to be tested under wartime conditions during the Spanish Civil War. They were powered by the Jumo 210 engine, a liquid-cooled inverted V-12 rated at 650hp for a top speed of 292mph. By the following spring, two squadrons were fighting in Spain with the Condor Legion. More followed, supporting General Franco's coup and learning valuable lessons that would be used to improve the fighter in the coming years.

The Bf 109C was a 'B' with more .30 cal. machine guns and a later model engine. The Bf 109D used a 900hp Daimler Benz 600A V-12 engine, a prototype of which dominated the 1937 Zurich

International Flying Meet, which was the first public showing of the Messerschmitt. This airplane, with a highly-modified engine of more than 1,600hp, later broke the World Speed Record for landplanes, with a series of low-altitude runs at almost 380mph.

Next to go into production was the first of the major versions, the Bf 109E, the prototype flying in mid-1938, and which was beginning to equip line squadrons in mid-1939. By the time Germany attacked Poland, the Bf 109E was its standard fighter, armed with two 20mm cannon and two .30 cal. machine guns. Top speed with an 1,100hp DB 601A V-12 was 354mph at 12,300ft, but cruising range was barely 400 miles. Versions of the E-model included a reconnaissance version, a longer-range version with a drop tank, and a ground-attack version for North African use, with increased armor to protect the engine.

It was the basic Bf 109E that met the Royal Air Force in the autumn of 1940, in what became known as the Battle of Britain. After a year of easily sweeping small air forces from the sky the Luftwaffe finally met its match. With pilots and airplanes the equal of any, RAF fighter squadrons took on a Luftwaffe that had never before seen its like. Guided by an effective radar warning system, Hurricanes and Spitfires littered the English landscape with wrecked Messerschmitts, as well as Heinkels and Junkers. Germany's goal of attaining aerial control over England was not reached, and so any plans for a cross-Channel invasion had to be shelved.

Modifications to the Bf 109E had been accompanied by added drag in the form of bulges and air intakes, and so the Bf 109F featured a more streamlined airframe which included a shallower supercharger intake and cantilever horizontal tail. A more powerful (1,300hp) DB 601E was installed on the prototype, which flew in July 1940 and entered action later that year. Armed with as many as three cannon and having a top speed of 390mph, it could outfly the Spitfire V at low and medium altitudes.

But the Germans continued to insist on experimenting with modifications that were adding weight and complications to an airplane that was working well. With ever-heavier armament and increased equipment, including cabin pressurization, the performance of the Bf 109G dropped below that of the Bf 109F. Nevertheless, the 'G' became the most heavily produced version, with more than 20,000 being built during 1943 and 1944, even though their inferiority to later-model Spitfires and the increasingly common P-51D Mustangs resulted in air battles being tilted increasingly in favor of the Allied fighters.

Two additional versions got as far as the advanced stages of testing, but not into large-scale production. The Bf 109H was a special high-altitude versions, its DB 60E engine and 6.5ft greater

Specifications of the Bf 109G-6

Length: 29ft 8in
Wingspan: 32ft 7in
Height: 8ft 6in
Wing area: 174 sq ft
Empty weight: 5,900lb
Maximum speed: 387mph at 23,000ft
Maximum range: 615 miles at 260mph at 19,000ft
Service ceiling: 38,500ft
Rate of climb: 3,300 ft/min

Surviving Examples

Bf 109E-1
Deutsches Museum

Bf 109E-3
Luftwaffe AJ+YM – Deutsches Museum
Deutsches Technikmuseum
1190 – Imperial War Museum (Duxford)
c/n 1342 – Flying Heritage Collection

Bf 109E-3a
Swiss J-355 – Swiss Air Force Museum

Bf 109E-3b
Luftwaffe 4101 – RAF Museum (Hendon)

Bf 109F
Russian Air Force Museum

wingspan enabling it to get up to 47,000ft. The Bf 109K was meant to compete with the much faster FW 190D and Ta 152, having a 1,550hp DB 605 engine equipped with nitrous oxide injection, the first time this was used. Its top speed of 450mph was achieved at 20,000ft , but the airplane appeared too late to see more than occasional action.

Two advanced designs were based on Bf 109 experience. The Me 209-II fighter (not to be confused with the Me 209V1 which was built strictly to win back the Absolute World Speed Record from Italy) was a follow-on to the Bf 109H, but bore little visual resemblance. Power was a 1,750hp Junkers Jumo inverted V-12; it carried three cannon and could top 450mph. But it was behind the FW 190D in development and did not get beyond the testing stage.

Bf 109F-2/Trop
South African National Museum of Military History
Luftwaffe 10639 – RAF Museum (Hendon)

Bf 109F-4/Z
Luftwaffe 101`32 – Canadian National Air Museum

Bf 109G-2
Yugoslav Aviation Museum
Luftwaffe 14658 – Northern Fleet Air Museum

Bf 109G-2/Trop
Luftwaffe 10639 – RAF Museum (Hendon)
Luftwaffe '14753' – Luftfahrtmuseum

Bf 109G-4
Luftwaffe 19310 – Technikmuseum

Bf 109G-6
Luftwaffe 10639 – RAF Museum (Hendon)

Bf 109-G-6/R3
Luftwaffe 160756 – US National Air & Space Museum

Bf-109G-6/U2
Luftwaffe 165227 – Central Air Museum of Finland

Bf 109G-6/Y
Luftwaffe 167271 – Central Air Museum of Finland

Bf 109G/8
Luftwaffe 411768 – Technical Museum, Moscow

Bf 109G-10/U4
Luftwaffe 610824 – National Museum of the US Air Force
Luftwaffe 610937 – Evergreen Aviation Museum

Messerschmitt Bf 110

Prof. Willy Messerschmitt was a great favorite of Adolf Hitler, and so his designs became symbols of the supremacy of the new Luftwaffe, even if not all of them deserved such lofty ranking. As long as Germany's early enemies such as Poland, the Netherlands and Belgium flew mid-1930s airplanes, supremacy was not a great challenge. But as the war moved on and the Allies began operating airplanes of equal or superior performance, some of the symbols became embarrassments.

The twin-engined fighter on which so much hope was placed was the Bf 110. The prototype, powered by a pair of DB 600 engines, first flew on 12 May 1936 and revealed a top speed of 315mph, slightly slower than the RAF's first Hawker Hurricane then undergoing tests. As the engines were not yet in mass production, the next four test models had 610hp Junkers Jumo 210B engines, with the result that the top speed dropped to 267mph, which would have made it a easy target.

By early 1938, the Daimler Benz factory was in full production of its more powerful engine, and so the Bf 110B used them, with a heavy (for the time) armament of two 20mm cannon and four .30 cal. machine guns. Plans to try the airplane out in the Spanish Civil War 'proving grounds' had to be cancelled when the peace treaty was signed. When the war began, Germany had a total of

fewer than 200 Bf 110s with front-line squadrons, but by the start of the Battle of Britain in the summer of 1940, more than 200 of the later Bf 110C were based in France near the English Channel coast. Operating from there, it was soon discovered by the Germans that their heavy fighters were no match for RAF Spitfires and Hurricanes so they withdrew them before they were all shot out of the sky.

The Bf 110D had considerably greater range, thanks to a large fixed fuel tank and ability to carry drop tanks. Its speed and maneuverability, however, were no greater and so it suffered the same fate as earlier versions. With the ability to carry a heavier bomb load, the Bf 110E was more of a light bomber, while the Bf

110F had an additional pair of 30mm cannon for its function as a bomber destroyer.

The next step involved a completely new airplane, the Me 210, development of which dated back to 1937. With a much cleaner airframe, 2,400hp DB 601 engines and a pair of remotely-controlled .50 cal. machine guns amidships and firing to the rear, it looked like a major improvement on the Bf 110. While 1,000 had been ordered even before the prototype had flown, a completely unacceptable accident rate led to early cancellation, and only 200 were delivered. An improved Me 310 with 1,750hp DB 603 engines and a pressurized cabin was planned but never built.

In view of the failure of its successor, Bf 110 production was reactivated, starting with the Bf 110G, which was produced in bomber-interceptor, heavy fighter, long-range reconnaissance, and the most common, night fighter versions with an elaborate series of aerials sticking out of the nose. The Bf 110H was built in parallel, with numerous improvements, most noticeably the installation of two 30mm cannon in the nose. These two versions were among the most widely produced, with more than 3,000 being built in 1943 and 1944.

Production finally ended in January 1945, outlasting even the considerably superior Me 410.

Specifications of the Bf 110G-4

Length: 41ft 7in
Wingspan: 53ft 5in
Height: 13ft 1in
Wing area: 413 sq ft
Empty weight: 11,220lb
Maximum speed: 342mph at 22,900ft
Maximum range: 1,300 miles with external fuel
Service ceiling: 26,000ft
Rate of climb: 7:54 to 18,000ft

Surviving Examples

Bf 110F-2
Luftwaffe 5052 – Deutsches Technikmuseum

Bf 110G-4/R-6
Luftwaffe 730301 – RAF Museum (Hendon)

Tank Ta 152

There is an impressive list of airplanes that showed promise of being the finest piston-engined fighter of World War Two, had they not come along too late to have any real impact. The final versions of the Spitfire and Spiteful are in this category, along with the North American P-51G and H, and the Martin-Baker MB.5. Add to that the German Ta 152.

Actually preceding the Ta 152 was the Ta 153, a FW 190 with a longer wing, DB 603 engine and many structural changes which, had it gone into production, would have required extensive and time-consuming re-tooling. It was cancelled after only test versions were built. The first Ta 152 was a slightly modified FW 190D with a 30mm cannon firing through the center of the propeller spinner. Only one of these was flown before the manufacturer moved on to the Ta 152B, which had a Jumo 213 engine with nitrous-oxide (NOx) injection that boosted its top sprint speed to 443mph at 44,000 feet, but it was never produced.

The Ta 152C had a stretched fuselage, larger tail surfaces, greater fuel capacity and four 20mm cannon. The first production version, equipped with both water-methanol and nitrous-oxide injection for brief dashes, could top out at 463mph at 33,000 feet. It did not become operational, despite the increasing desperation of the Luftwaffe, which was having difficulties coping with the latest British and American fighters.

The Ta 152E was a photo-reconnaissance version, of which few were built and none saw action. It was the Ta 152H, with its wings extended from the standard 36 feet to 47.5 feet that showed the true potential of the design. Construction consisted of modifying FW 190 airframes, and while production began in November 1944, only 10 were flown before the war ended, a half year later.

Among the proposed developments that never came to pass were a low-altitude fighter with a 3,000hp Jumo V-12 engine and a radial-engined sub-type with a four-stage supercharger. One can't help but wonder if the factory had spent less effort and time on experiments and proposals, it might have been able to build more airplanes.

Specifications of the Ta 152H

Wingspan: 47ft 7in
Height: 13ft 0in
Wing area: 253 sq ft
Empty weight: 9,060lb
Maximum speed: 431mph at 35,000ft
Maximum range: 745 miles at 372mph at 32,800ft
Service ceiling: 48,560
Rate of Climb: 3,300 ft/min

Surviving Example

Ta 152H
Luftwaffe 150020 – US National Air & Space Museum

Blohm & Voss BV 155

This bomber-cum-fighter from Messerschmitt-cum-Blohm & Voss was emblematic of the turmoil within the accelerating collapse of Germany's Nazi government, and of the bizarre feeling in some parts of its aircraft industry that something almost magical was going to happen to prolong or even win the war, despite overwhelming evidence to the contrary.

The BV 155 began life in 1942 as the Messerschmitt Me 155, a design for a carrier-based single-seat fighter using the fuselage of a Bf 109G and a new wing and 1,475hp DB 605A V-12 engine. It was to have had an unusually wide-spaced main landing gear, no doubt in hopes of curing the severe ground-looping tendencies of the that plagued the Bf 109 and resulted in hundreds of accidents. This quickly lost favor and, in fact, no such purpose-built fighter was ever produced.

Then it became a fast high-altitude bomber, the Me 155A, but still failed to elicit much official enthusiasm. The third incarnation was as the Me 155B, a high-altitude fighter, but with Messerchmitt busy building other, more promising airplanes, the project was handed off to Blohm & Voss and re-designated the BV 155B. The wings

were modified, with the outboard Bf 109 wing panels attached to a new, longer center section which stretched the wingspan to an amazing 68ft 11in, the greatest of any World War Two fighter.

Just as striking were the radiators, enclosed in large streamlined nacelles halfway between the wing roots and wing tips and looking for all the world as if they could have contained engines. Before the prototype flew, it had received a redesigned wing with a laminar flow airfoil. By the time the BV 155V1 prototype was ready for its first test, it was February 1945, and the walls were closing in on the Third Reich.

Further changes reduced the wingspan of the fourth prototype to 61ft 2in, and, with a new type of supercharger, the engine power was boosted to 1,800hp. The performance of this version was estimated to include a top speed of 428mph at 50,000ft. But all this was little more than a pipe-dream, as the planned first flight in the middle of April 1945, fell victim to the final Allied advances into the heart of Germany. The order for the remainder of 30 test models was never filled, and the sole surviving prototype was soon on its way to America and, eventually, the Smithsonian Institution's National Air Museum.

Specifications of the BV 155V-2

Length: 39ft 5in
Wingspan: 67ft 3in
Height: 9ft 10in
Wing area: 420 sq ft
Empty weight: 10,735lb
Maximum speed: 429mph at 52,500ft estimated
Maximum range: 930 miles

Service ceiling: 55,600ft estimated
Rate of climb: 29:00 to 52,300ft

Surviving Example

BV 155V-2
Luftwaffe 360052 – US National Air & Space Museum

Heinkel He 162 Salamander
The little Heinkel was one of military history's great examples of desperation. It was created in amazingly little time, rushed into production before being properly tested, built in quantity, and yet failed to have any impact on the war, as it was never seen in combat.

The specifications for a lightweight jet fighter using minimal critical materials was announced in September 1944. A mock-up was shown to government officials two weeks later, and the airplane was ordered into mass production less than a week after that! The first prototype flew in early December but soon crashed during a high-speed demonstration, killing Heinkel's chief test pilot when its wood-bonding adhesive failed and the wing came apart. Still, the goal of 1,000 airplanes per month was seen as attainable, and was soon increased to 3,000 when a second major factory was brought into the program.

Due to the heavy impact of Allied bombing raids on aircraft production, many of the large and small factories involved in building He 162s were underground, where many hundreds of unfinished airplanes were discovered when they were overrun by Allied army units. The severe lack of pilots and of safe facilities in which to train new ones caused men as young as 14 to be conscripted into training units, given a few flights in clipped-wing gliders to simulate the experience of landing an He 162, and immediately rushed into flying high-performance jets. As one such student later told the author, 'I was just a kid. What did I know? It was fun!'

Of an estimated 160 Heinkels that were delivered to Luftwaffe fighter squadrons, not one is known to have gotten into action.

Specifications of the He 162A

Length: 29ft 9in
Wingspan: 23ft 8in
Height: 8ft 6in
Wing area: 120 sq ft
Maximum weight: 5,940lb
Maximum speed: 522mph at 20,000ft

Maximum range: 410 miles
Service ceiling: 36,000ft+
Rate of climb: 4,230ft/min

Surviving Examples

He 162A-1
Luftwaffe 120235 – Imperial War Museum (London)

He 162A-2
Luftwaffe 120077 – Planes of Fame
Luftwaffe 120223 – Musee de l'Air
Luftwaffe 120230 – US National Air & Space Museum
Luftwaffe 120076, 120086 – Canadian National Museum
Luftwaffe 120227 – RAF Museum (Hendon)

Messerschmitt Me 163 Komet

The Komet was, by almost any standard, the most unusual military airplane ever to see combat. It was the world's first (and probably last) solely rocket-powered fighter, and while its performance was spectacular and thus highly intimidating, it had little measurable impact on the outcome of the war. Its superior speed and rate of climb were more than balanced out by serious practical shortcomings which might have been eliminated had it not been rushed into operation before it was ready. With enough fuel for just a few minutes of engine run, it was relegated to point-defense of particularly vital targets

It started out as a research airplane designed by Prof. Alexander Lippisch, who saw it as a test-bed for rocket motors. It was only when an early powered flight of the Me 163A prototype in August

1941 produced a speed of 570mph – 100mph over the existing World Speed Record – that its potential as an interceptor received serious consideration. Soon afterwards, an air-launch resulted in a clocked speed of 624mph, and its redesign into a combat airplane was begun.

The original Helmut Walter rocket engine had serious problems, including highly varying thrust. This was soon corrected by an engine of more than double the power and more reliable operation. Even with the addition of considerable military equipment, the new Me 163B had a top speed just short of 600mph. This advantage of some 150mph over the Allies' fastest fighters would give it an edge rarely seen in war.

Despite the Luftwaffe's increasingly desperate need for superior fighters, the first unit equipped with Me 163B was not formed until June 1944, shortly after the Allies' invasion of France. It was another two months before they were seen in action against a daylight raid by American B-17s. Due to having a powered flight duration of just a few minutes, the usual tactic was to blast to high speed and then coast, and soon bomber formations were seeing them knife down through at double the bombers' speed, fire air-to-air rockets and then climb back up again in preparation for another attack.

The Me 163 may have been impossible to counter in the air, but when it came time to landing and refueling, its novel undercarriage comprised of a wheeled dolly that was dropped just after take-off and a non-retractable landing skid was a major handicap. There was a strong chance that when the landing skid first scraped along the concrete runway, sparks would ignite any remaining fuel and produce a fireball where once there had been an airplane. Only about 350 Komets were built, though parts for many hundreds more were discovered by the Allies after the war, hidden in underground factories, intended to be impervious to conventional bombing.

The Me 163C was to have had a more powerful motor, more fuel, and a pressurized cockpit, along with a load of two 30mm cannon and 24 unguided air-to-air rockets. The test program had barely begun when the war ended. Beyond that, the Me 263A was to have had retractable landing gear, a 4,400lb Walter motor, more fuel and thus greater duration of flight. Plans to put it into large-scale production were still being made when Germany surrendered.

Specifications of the Me 163B-1a

Length: 18ft 8in
Wingspan: 30ft 7in
Height: 9ft 0in
Wing area: 211 sq ft
Empty weight: 4,200lb
Maximum speed: 596mph at 10,000–30,000ft
Maximum endurance: 8 min
Service ceiling: 39,500ft
Rate of climb: 16,000ft/min

Surviving Examples

Me 163B-1a
Luftwaffe 191095 – National Museum of the USAF
Luftwaffe 191301 – US National Air & Space Museum
Luftwaffe 191916 – Canadian National Air Museum
Luftwaffe 191309 or 191912 – Deutsches Museum
Luftwaffe 191316 – Science Museum (London)
Luftwaffe 191614 – RAF Museum (Cosford)
Luftwaffe 191659 – Scottish Museum of Flight
Luftwaffe 191904 – Luftwaffe Museum
Luftwaffe 191907 – Australian War Memorial
Luftwaffe 191660 – Flying Heritage Collection

Focke Wulf FW 190

It was widely considered to be the finest piston-engined German fighter produced in quantity during World War Two, and rivaled the P-51D Mustang in overall performance. Twenty-thousand were built, with the first flying in June 1939, shortly before the war started. It had a 14-cylinder, two-row, air-cooled BMW radial engine rated at 1,550hp, and an unusually large spinner having a hole in the center for cooling air. This reduced the airflow and led to over-heating and was soon removed so a conventional cowl could be used.

During testing of several prototypes, a newer BMW engine was installed, the cockpit moved aft to counterbalance the heavier engine, and wings with greater span and area adopted, as they improved maneuverability. The first production FW 190As appeared in late 1940, and by early 1941, 100 had been delivered,

with pilot complaints leading to the addition of two 20mm cannon to the original armament of four .30 cal. machine guns.

The first FW 190As went into action in the summer of 1941 from captured French airfields along the English Channel coast, where they clearly out-performed the RAF's Spitfire Mk.Vs. Steady increases in power from the same basic BMW801 produced speeds over 400mph. For brief bursts of power, some versions were equipped for nitrous oxide or water-methanol injection, which added several hundred horsepower.

The FW 190 was destined to replace the Messerschmitt Bf 109 as the Luftwaffe's primary fighter and fighter-bomber, with production soon outpacing the slower, older design. It controlled western European skies until the Spitfire IX, of equal performance, appeared in the autumn of 1942. The need for a version having much better high-altitude capability led to the FW 190B with an extended nose housing an 1800hp DB601 liquid-cooled inverted V-12 engine inside a cowling that made it appear to have a radial engine, and a pressurized cockpit which permitted flight well above 40,000 feet.

Before the FW 190B could complete its testing, it was replaced by the FW 190D with an even longer nose and an 1,800hp Jumo V-12 engine. Top speed was increased to 425mph at 22,000 feet, while the armament was two 20mm cannon and two .50 cal. machine guns. By the time the war ended, production totaled 13,367 fighters and 6,634 fighter-bombers. The final version of the design was the Ta 152 long-nosed fighter, re-designated to honor designer Kurt Tank.

Specifications of the FW 190A-8

Length: 29ft 0in
Wingspan: 34ft 6in
Height: 13ft 0in
Wing area: 197 sq ft
Empty weight: 7,000lb
Maximum speed: 408mph at 20,600ft
Maximum range: 500 miles on internal fuel
Service ceiling: 37,400ft
Rate of climb: 2,350ft / min

Surviving Examples

FW 190A-3
Luftwaffe 132219 – Royal Norwegian Air Museum

FW 190A-5
Biggin Hill Airfield Museum

FW 190A-6
Luftwaffe 550214 – South African Museum of Military History
Lubbock, Texas

FW 190A-8
Luftwaffe 730924 – Musee de l'Air (built in France as an NC-900)
Luftwaffe 733682 – Imperial War Museum (London)

FW 190A-8/R6
Luftwaffe 733682 – Imperial War Museum (London)

FW 190D-9
Luftwaffe Air Museum,
Luftwaffe 601088 – National Museum of the US Air Force

FW 190D-13
Luftwaffe 836017 – Flying Heritage Collection

FW 190F-8
Kissimmee Fla.,

FW 190F-8/R1
Luftwaffe 931884 – US National Air & Space Museum

FW 190F-8/U1
Luftwaffe 584219 – RAF Museum (Hendon)
c/n 62 – Musee de l'Air (Paris)

Heinkel He 219 Uhu

The development of German twin-engined fighters that began with the marginally-successful Messerschmitt Bf 110 led eventually to the He 219, whose performance and potential for carrying out a variety of tasks could not be realized due to a lack of skilled workmen, German insistence on developing a wide range of versions, and destructive raids on production facilities.

Development of the 219 began in August 1940, as a proposal for a high-speed light bomber and torpedo plane that was converted into a fighter. Serious design was begun in January 1942, but was interrupted when a raid by RAF bombers destroyed all the drawings. Finally, the prototype He 219V-1 flew in November 1942, and exhibited impressive flying qualities. It initially was armed with two 20mm cannon in a tray under the fuselage, plus

a single .50 cal. machine gun firing from the rear cockpit. To this was soon added four 30mm cannon, and some test models had six 20mm cannon.

By early 1943, the total order for He 219s was up to 300, and three more factories were building major components. In June several test airplanes were engaged in trials under what was called 'operational conditions', which included actual combat. Claims were made during this period that He 219 pilots had shot down many British airplanes, several of which were said to have been previously-immune Mosquitos.

Almost 30 airplanes were designated prototypes and used to test a wide range of modifications and combinations of guns and engines. One was armed with two 30mm cannon firing at an upward angle to enable it to fly under an enemy airplane and shoot at it from below. In July the German Air Ministry demanded delivery of 24 He 219s per month, while only an average of 10 could be supplied because of a shortage of skilled workmen.

Among the proposed versions were one with 1,900hp engines that could carry more than a ton of bombs, and a high-altitude reconnaissance-bomber having a wingspan of 86ft 11in, two of which were under construction when they were destroyed by bombing raids. Several designs were tried with a second cockpit before production was ordered stopped in May 1944. This was ignored, with a half dozen 'unofficial' He 219s being assembled from spare parts.

In November 1944, additional effort was placed on the production of fighters, though the He 219 was excluded. Nevertheless, production continued apparently without official authorization until the two main factories in Poland were caught up in the Soviet advance. Still, new versions continued to appear until the

very last minute, with the He 219B-2 intended expressly to attack Mosquitos, a few of which found their way into action, along with more prototypes that had been pressed into use. Even the He 219C saw the light of day, if only briefly. It had a crew of four, including a tail gunner, and was designed to use 2,500hp Jumo engines and carry a bomb load of 3,300lb, clearly taking it out of the fighter category. At war's end, the first two were still waiting for engines to be delivered.

Even though it was in production for a considerable time, only 268 airplanes plus 20 prototypes got to operational squadrons. Despite its superior performance, it received a much lower priority than airplanes it might logically have replaced.

Specifications of the He 219A

Length: 31ft 0in
Wingspan: 60ft 9in
Height: 13ft 6in
Wing area: 479 sq ft
Empty weight: 24,700lb
Maximum speed: 415mph at 23,000ft
Maximum range: 1,250 miles
Absolute ceiling: 41,650ft
Rate of climb: 1,800ft/min

Surviving Example

He 219A
Luftwaffe GI+KQ – US National Air & Space Museum

Messerschmitt Me 262 Schwalbe (Swallow)

When it came to the Me 262 Swallow, the German military's reputation for organizational efficiency was nowhere to be seen. The world's first jet fighter can be traced back to 1938 and a contract to Messerschmitt for a flying test-bed for new turbojet engines from Junkers and BMW. It didn't get into combat until July 1944, thanks to mechanical shortcomings, Allied bombings and a puzzling shortage of coordinated high-level enthusiasm.

The first German jet engines had service lifetimes measured in minutes, which made it difficult for test pilots to learn much about their airplane's design and construction. The first test flight with jet engines only, was in July 1942. And while that airplane was destroyed a few weeks later, the government ordered 45 more.

Take-off acceleration was so poor that a pair of 1,100lb booster rockets were used to get the airplanes off the ground.

Progress would no doubt have been a lot quicker had the full support of Hitler been applied. But he still insisted that most Me 262s be equipped for ground-support use as a light bomber, where its superior top speed was of little advantage, rather than as an interceptor. Even when the full capabilities of the fighter had finally been recognized by high officials, mass production was slow in coming, though part of the reason was the destruction of a great quantity of its specialized tooling in an air attack on the factory at Regensburg in August 1943.

Even though a great many airplanes were lost due to the prevailing view that the Me 262 was easy to fly, a two-seat trainer version did not make its appearance until late 1944 when the

quality of new pilots was hitting new lows. Several trainers were then modified into two-seat night fighters – Me 262B-1a – which led to the Me 262B-2a. While more than 1,400 Me 262s were built, barely 200 got into squadrons as fighters, thus the airplane had a limited impact on the conduct of the war.

In fact, some authorities claim that more Me 262s were lost to slower but more maneuverable Allied fighters than the jets were able to claim in response. Scores of Me 262s were shot down while taking off or landing, as their poor acceleration made them defenseless targets.

The true impact of the radical Messerschmitt was long-term, with all air forces quickly becoming convinced that the future of air warfare lay in the turbojet-powered combat airplane. Its far greater speed, combined with the vast potential for power increases, along

Surviving Examples

Me 262A-1a
National Museum of the USAF
Luftwaffe 500491 –US National Air & Space Museum
Deutsches Museum

Me 262A-1b
Luftwaffe 500071 – Deutsches Museum
Luftwaffe 111617 – Planes of Fame

Me 262A-2a
Luftwaffe 112372 – RAF Museum (Hendon)
Luftwaffe 500200 – Australian War Museum

Me 262B-1a
Luftwaffe 110305 – South African National Museum of Military History
Luftwaffe 110639 – NAS Willow Grove, Pa.

Avia S.92 (Czech-built Me 262A-1)
Prague-Kbely

with the reduced maintenance for the far simpler propulsion system, accelerated the inevitable complete replacement of the piston engines which had been aviation's stand-by since 1903.

Specifications of the Me 262A-1a

Length: 34ft 10in
Wingspan: 41ft 0in
Height: 12ft 7in
Wing area: 234 sq ft
Empty weight: 9,740lb
Maximum speed: 540mph at 19,700ft
Maximum range: 650 miles at 29,600ft
Service ceiling: 37,570ft
Rate of climb: 3,940ft/min

Dornier Do 335

Perhaps the most radical propeller-driven fighter of the war, the Do 335 packed two 1,900hp DB 601 V-12s into the extremities of its fuselage, thus eliminating the need for drag-producing separate nacelles.

It began as the Do 331 fighter-bomber in 1941, then was cancelled when Luftwaffe needs changed. This delayed the first flight into late 1943, though orders had already been placed for 14 test models, 10 pre-production airplanes, a production run of 11 Do 335A-1s and 2 two-seat trainers. To speed up the test program in late 1944, the pre-production airplanes were added to the 14 prototypes. The usual wide variety of variations was experimented with, including two-seat night fighters and reconnaissance versions, with a second cockpit located behind and above the first.

The first production machines were delivered to Luftwaffe units in early 1945, but exhibited serious instability at high speed, and only 10 made it that far.

The Do 335B was to have been a fighter armed with no fewer than three 30mm cannon and two 20mm cannon. As Allied armies closed in, the Dornier works was still planning numerous versions of the airplane, including one with special 2,100hp high-altitude engines and wings with 15 feet greater span. These and many other fascinating schemes came to naught, as Germany's enemies took over the factory. Of the 10 Do 335As delivered, none was ever reported seen in combat. The sole survivor, a Do 335A-O2, was captured, taken to the USA and transferred to the National Air & Space Museum. It was restored by and briefly displayed at the Deutsches Museum in Germany.

The ultimate development of the Do 335 was to have been the Do 635, a very large craft with two Do 335 fuselages on one stretched wing in the style of the P-82 Twin Mustang. It was estimated to have a maximum range of some 4,000 miles, which was many times what was required for any imaginable mission in its day, unless someone was dreaming of a one-way flight to the east coast of the United States, where it would drop its half-ton bomb load and win the war! In some ways, the Germans were as far out of touch with reality at the end of the war as the French had been at the beginning.

Specifications of the Do 335A-1

Length: 45ft 5in
Wingspan: 45ft 3in
Height: 16ft 5in
Wing area: 414 sq ft
Empty weight: 16,315lb
Maximum speed: 413mph at 26,200ft
Maximum range: 2,330 miles at 385mph at 19,700ft with 630-gallon external tank
Service ceiling: 37,400ft
Rate of climb: 3,600 ft/min

Surviving Example

Do 335A-02
Luftwaffe VG+PH, 240102; USAAF FE-505 – US National Air & Space Museum

Bachem Ba 349 Natter
No doubt the most unusual concept for a World War Two fighter to advance to multiple test flights, the Natter was a pure 'point defense' type intended to guard specific facilities of particular sensitivity from air attack. Had it been available in sufficient numbers, and while there was still something left in Germany worth attacking, it might have made a difference. Neither of these requirements came close to being met.

It pioneered several ideas that later became accepted. It took off as a 'tail-sitter', blasting vertically into the sky with four 1,100lb solid-fuel rockets that could be jettisoned when their fuel had been burned. It was armed exclusively with two dozen 2in diameter air-to-air rockets. Once its mission had been completed, its cockpit, including the pilot, could be disconnected from the rest of the airplane and returned to earth via parachute.

The first test flight was made from the secret test base at Peenemunde, on the Baltic Sea, in late 1944 as a glider towed aloft by a He 111 bomber. This was followed by a series of launchings of the airframe without the pilot and without the main rocket motor. In late February 1945, one was sent off with its main motor, but still pilotless. Finally, a few days later, the first test flight of the complete airplane was made and promptly cost Germany one of its rapidly dwindling supply of trained test pilots.

The flyability of the Ba 349 was demonstrated with three successful test flights, and by April the first batch of three dozen production machines had been finished. Ten of them were soon in place at Kircheim in expectation of a formation of American daylight bombers to allow them to prove themselves in combat. Before that could happen, American soldiers captured the launching sites and put an end to the novel experiment.

One improved Ba 349B prototype was flown, demonstrating a top speed of 620mph and a rate of climb of 37,400ft/min. But like the entire program, it was simply too little and too late.

Specifications for the Ba 349A

Length: 21ft 3in
Wingspan: 13ft 1in
Height: 8ft 6in
Wing area: 52 sq ft
Loaded weight: 4,800lb
Maximum speed: 560mph at 16,400ft
Maximum endurance: 2 minutes
Service ceiling: 46,000 ft
Rate of climb: 35,800ft/min

Surviving Example

Ba 349A-1
USAAF FE-1 – US National Air & Space Museum
Deutsches Museum

Messerschmitt Me 410

Efforts to replace the increasingly outdated Bf 110 twin-engine heavy fighters which were being shot down by the score were stymied by serious problems with planned replacements.

The Me 210 was a highly modified Bf 110, with more powerful engines, a single vertical tail and a general aerodynamic clean-up. Problems persisted, however, and when 1,000 were ordered before the prototype had flown, the seeds of its demise had been sown. An unacceptable accident rate could not be eased by additional modifications, and so production was ended before half of the planned number had been delivered. The Me 310 was cancelled while it was still on the drawing board.

Finally, the Me 410 was ordered in late 1942. The first ones had two fixed 20mm cannon and two .30 cal. machine guns, along with single .50 cal. machine guns in remote-controlled barbettes on either side of the fuselage, facing rearward. Later, two more 20mm cannon were added. Actually a fighter-bomber, it could carry up to 4,400lb of bombs.

The Me 410 was not a top-priority program, as only 290 were delivered in 1943, and another 720 in 1944. Limited production in occupied Hungary ended when the factory was destroyed by an air raid in 1944. Despite the increased power and resultant greater performance, the Me 410 was no more effective than the Bf 110. But by the time of its end, Messerschmitt was concentrating on the far superior Me 262 jet fighter. Interest in advanced piston-engined fighters was consigned to the history books.

Specifications of the Me 410B

Length: 40ft 11in
Wingspan: 53ft 8in
Height: 14ft 1in
Wing area: 390 sq ft
Empty weight: 13,550lb
Maximum speed: 388mph at 22,000ft
Maximum range: 1,450 miles
Service ceiling: 32,800ft
Rate of climb: 10:42 to 22,000ft

Surviving Examples

Me 410A-1
Luftwaffe 420430 – RAF Museum (Cosford)

Me 410A-2
Lutwaffe F6+WK – US National Air & Space Museum

Chapter Twelve

Italy

Fiat CR.32

It was the last production Italian pursuit plane whose speed took a back seat to its aerobatic capabilities, a testament to the long-term influence of World War I dogfights. Its origins date back to Fiat's CR.1 in the early 1920s and led to a successful line of pursuits culminating in the CR.42.

The CR.32, an improvement on the CR.30, first flew in prototype form in 1933, continuing the use of diagonal inter-plane bracing, characteristic of Celestino Rosatelli-designed biplanes. More than 380 of the initial version, powered by the 600hp inverted V-12 Fiat A.30 engine, and armed with two .50 cal. machine guns, were produced before being replaced on the assembly lines by the CR.32bis, which added two .30 cal. machine guns. More than 300 of these were built, making it one of the major production runs of the day.

It received its baptism of fire in the early days of the Spanish Civil War, in 1936, equipping resident Spanish Nationalist air units as well as Italian Air Force squadrons sent to help the Franco forces.

The third version – CR.32ter – appeared in 1936 and differed little from its predecessors. When 100 had been delivered, the final CR.32quater took its place to become the most common, with almost 450 built through late 1939. Some of these were modified for use as night fighters. And in 1938, the Spanish produced them

as the HA.132.L 'Chirri'. As the CR.32 ended its production run it was replaced by the more powerful, better streamlined CR.42 Falco.

When World War Two began, 175 CR.32s remained in Italian Air Force service, the last of them being retired in the spring of 1941 after service throughout the eastern Mediterranean.

Specifications of the CR.32

Length: 24ft 5in
Wingspan: 31ft 2in
Height: 8ft 11in
Wing area: 238 sq ft
Empty weight: 3,040lb
Maximum speed: 221mph at 9,850ft
Maximum range: 485 miles
Service ceiling: 25,750ft
Rate of climb: 2,200ft/min

Surviving Examples

CR.32
Spain C1-262 – Museo del Aire
MM '4667' – Italian Air Force Museum

Fiat CR.42 Falco (Falcon)

As the last biplane pursuit in production by any of the countries involved in World War Two, it was already obsolete when the fighting began, yet remained in service for more than a year. The Italian Air Force was the last major air arm to admit that the monoplane was the shape of the future and that any remaining biplanes should be retired to non-combat duties.

The Falco was one of the most beautiful military biplanes ever produced, and while it owes much to its immediate predecessor, the CR.32, the resemblance is minimal aside from the diagonal inter-plane bracing. The first prototype flew in early 1939 when Germany was building Bf 109s, and Britain was building

Hurricanes and Spitfires. Within months, production airplanes were coming off the assembly line, powered by an 840hp Fiat A.74 two-row radial engine and carrying one .30 cal. and one .50 cal. machine gun. This was soon changed to two .50 cal., and then to four .50 cal. machine guns as contemporary reports of air combat involving heavily armed fighters and bombers were studied.

The first air force to place the CR.42 in action was that of Hungary, not long after Germany had invaded Poland in the late summer of 1939. At the same time, Belgium ordered 34 pursuits, the first of which were assigned to squadrons in May 1940. Sweden followed suit with an order for 72 pursuits powered by license-built Bristol Mercury engines. In June 1940, the Italian Air Force threw Falcos into action against French D.520s and used them in raids on England in late 1940. The losses incurred in the latter actions should have convinced the Italians to pull the CR.42 out of

combat, but it continued to be used in North African operations. It was finally relegated to the ground-attack role, even though its bomb load was limited to 440lb.

In an effort to bring its performance up to that of its enemies, Fiat experimented in 1941 with the CR.42B having a 1,000hp DB 601 V-12 engine which boosted its top speed by more than 50mph. But it still had two wings and far too many external struts and wires. Production continued until 1942, at which time almost 1,800 had been built. All future Fiat fighters, however, would be monoplanes.

Specifications for the CR.42

Length: 27ft 3in
Wingspan: 31ft 10in
Height: 10ft 10in
Wing area: 241 sq ft
Empty weight: 3,765lb
Maximum speed: 266mph at 13,120ft
Maximum range: 630 miles at 214mph at 19,700ft with 26-gallon external tank
Service ceiling: 33,300ft
Rate of climb: 3,100 ft/min

Surviving Examples

CR.42
MM5701 – RAF Museum (Hendon)
Civil G-CBLS – Imperial War Museum (Duxford)
MM'4653' – Italian Air Force Museum
(J11) Fv.2543 – Flygvapenmuseum

Fiat G.50 Freccia (Arrow)

An Italian government specification, issued in 1936, produced prototypes of several important designs, including the Macchi MC.200 and Reggiane Re.2000, as well as the Fiat G.50. All were monoplanes, and flew before the CR.42 biplane, and easily outperformed the CR.42, yet the latter went into production and service alongside them.

The G.50 prototype made its first flight in February 1937, a full two years before that of the CR.42. It had the same pair of .50 cal. machine guns as the others, and saw its first action in Spain in 1938, almost a year before the CR.42 and two years before the others. Despite being underpowered by an 840hp Fiat A.74 two-row radial engine, a dozen were sent to Spain for realistic combat testing. The government was generally pleased with the results, and ordered another 200 with open cockpits to fit pilots' complaints that they could not feel the wind against their faces.

Finland ordered 35 G.50s in 1939, but they were grabbed by the Germans and held until the end of the Russo–Finnish War, when they were released to the Finns. Upon Italy's entry into the war in June 1940, almost 50 were stationed in occupied Belgium, but were never reported in combat. G.50s subsequently went into action in Greece and then throughout the Mediterranean theater of war.

Acceptance by pilots of the G.50 was lukewarm, due to its lack of offensive weapons and limited performance. Attempts to improve this led to tests of the G.50ter, with a 1,000hp Fiat engine which provided greater speed, but still not enough to cope with the increasingly powerful Allied fighters and bombers. A planned version with a DB 6012A V-12 engine became the G.52, which was dropped when the much improved G.55 made its debut in mid-1942.

Specifications of the G.50bis

Length: 27ft 2in
Wingspan: 36ft 1in
Height: 9ft 2in
Wing area: 196 sq ft
Empty weight: 4,440lb
Maximum speed: 293mph at 16,400ft
Maximum range: 630 miles
Service ceiling: 32,480ft
Rate of climb: 8:00 to 16,400ft

Surviving Examples

G.50
Croat 3505, ex-MM6182 – Italian Air Force Museum
Italian Air Force MM6197 – Air Museum of Belgrade

Fiat G.55 Centauro (Centaur)

Italian fighters in operation prior to the middle of the war all suffered from a serious lack of speed and of firepower, thus were easily dealt with by British and American fighters. Starting in mid-1943, an extensively modified version of the G.50 began to emerge. The G.55 prototype first flew in April 1942, with production starting a year later. It looked more like a Bf 109 than previous Fiat fighters.

While obviously a descendant of the G.50, it boasted increased size, increased power, increased armament and much increased performance. With a 1,475hp Fiat R.A. 1050 inverted V-12 engine (license-built DB 601A) and far superior streamlining, it could fly almost 100mph faster, climb quicker and fly much higher. It was initially fitted with a single 20mm cannon in addition to four .50 cal. machine guns, but soon added two more cannon, to give it a fully modern array of guns.

Production began in August 1943, and less than a month later, the Italian government surrendered to the Allies, turning over the central and southern parts of the country. As production of the G.55 was based in Turin, in the north, it remained under German control, and, with the exception of a few airplanes, all those ordered were assigned to units of the Reggia Aeronautica that remained on the German side. Several thousand were ordered, but only 100 had been completed by the time all of Italy was freed.

Proposed advanced versions of the G.55 included the G.55/II with five 20mm cannon, and the G.55S which was to have carried a torpedo. After the war, production was restarted and almost 100 more were built for export.

Specifications of the G.55

Length: 31ft 1in
Wingspan: 38ft 11in
Height: 10ft 6in
Wing area: 227 sq ft
Empty weight: 6,393lb
Maximum speed: 426mph at 22,965ft
Maximum range: 795 miles
Service ceiling: 43,965ft
Rate of climb: 3,300 ft/min

Surviving Example

G.55
MM53265 – Italian Air Force Museum

Macchi MC.200 Saetta (Arrow)

Visually, it was almost identical to the Fiat G.50, distinguishable mainly by the streamlined bumps around the engine cowling. While its performance was no better, pilots preferred it due to its superior maneuverability and gentle handling characteristics, which probably should have made it a better sport airplane than a fighter.

Following the Italian war against Ethiopia in the late 1930s, the Reggia Aeronautica embarked on an expansion program which was to involve 3,000 new airplanes of all categories. Winner of the 1938 government competition for a new interceptor was the Macchi MC.200, designed by Mario Castoldi, whose earlier MC.72 still holds the World Speed Record for piston-engined seaplanes at 441mph. Weighing but 3,900lb empty, the first MC.200 was powered by an 870hp, 14-cylinder Fiat A.74

The first production machines were rejected by one squadron's pilots who preferred to stick with their more maneuverable biplanes, and other pilots objected to the closed cockpit canopy, which was then replaced by an open one.

By the time Italy declared war on the Allies in June 1940, more than 150 Saetta were on strength with squadrons. There is no evidence that they took part in any actions against the French prior to France's surrender, having been grounded following crashes that were eventually blamed on high-speed stalls, which were soon corrected by changes to the wing's airfoil shape. With this change, the MC.200 became one of the better Italian fighters of the war, possessing maneuverability superior to all Allied fighters.

Due to its limited speed and firepower, however, it could not stand up against the likes of Spitfires, Hurricanes and Mustangs. It was used, instead, in the escort role for S.M.79 tri-motored bombers

and German Ju 87 Stuka dive bombers. Two groups served on the Eastern Front against the Red Air Force. Others were used as fighter-bombers, carrying up to 700lb of bombs. Of 1,000 built, a few served with squadrons that had survived Italy's capitulation to the Allies.

Specifications of the MC.200

Length: 26ft 11in
Wingspan: 34ft 9in
Height: 11ft 6in
Wing area: 181 sq ft
Empty weight: 4,175lb
Maximum speed: 312mph at 14,750ft
Maximum range: 540 miles at 280mph
Service ceiling: 29,200ft
Rate of climb: 3,200ft/min

Surviving Examples

MC.200
MM8307 ('MM7707') – Italian Air Force Museum
MM8146 – National Museum of the US Air Force

Macchi MC.202 Folgore (Thunderbolt)

This airplane is generally regarded as the most effective Italian fighter of World War Two, due to its performance and widespread use. A direct development of the radial-engined MC.200, it used the same fuselage, wings and tail, which were married to a 1,175hp Alfa Romeo R.A. 1000, which was a license-built DB 601 V-12.

The prototype first flew in August 1940, and so pleased Reggia Aeronautica officials that it was immediately ordered into large-scale production, pilot's antiquated preferences for open cockpits finally having subsided. At first, armament consisted of just two .50 cal. machine guns, but they were soon augmented by either two .30 cal. machine guns or a pair of 20mm cannon. A bomb load of up to 660lb could be carried under the wings.

Folgores first entered the war in November 1941, in North Africa, where they demonstrated their superiority to the P-40 and Hurricane. Others went into action on the Russian front. Despite the total production of 1,500 MC.202 airframes, operations were limited by the inability of Alfa Romeo to deliver engines in the numbers needed. As a result, the inferior MC.200 remained in production.

Construction of the MC.202 was, if anything, of higher quality than needed. The author was once told by a member of the Smithsonian Institution's restoration team working on an MC.202 that the airplane must have been built by men who had previously worked for Ferrari.

Specifications of the MC.202

Length: 29ft 1in
Wingspan: 34ft 9in
Height: 10ft 0in
Wing area: 181 sq ft
Empty weight: 5,180lb
Maximum speed: 370mph at 17,400ft
Maximum range: 475 miles
Service ceiling: 37,730ft
Rate of climb: 3,900 ft/min

Surviving Examples

MC.202
USAAF FE-498 and 'MM9476' – US National Air & Space Museum
'MM7844' – Italian Air Force Museum

Macchi MC.205 Veltro (Greyhound)

The next step in the development of a truly modern Italian fighter was the MC.205, which was basically an MC.202 airframe with an Alfa Romeo-built DB 605, which produced another 300hp. This raised the top speed of the MC.205 by 30mph, but the added weight seriously reduced its rate of climb. The first few built had two .30 cal. and two .50 cal. machine guns, while most had two .50 cal. and two 20mm cannon, still not an overwhelming array of firepower. Regardless, it was able to meet the best of Allied fighters on fairly even terms for the first time. Production, however, was limited to a few hundred before Italy signed the armistice with the Allies.

The MC.205V was first seen in action in July 1943, escorting torpedo bombers which were attacking Allied naval forces. Two months later, Italy's Fascist government surrendered. Only 66 Veltros had been assigned to squadrons, and barely half of those were available for use. A few joined the Allies, while the bulk of them joined squadrons loyal to Nazi Germany.

Only 262 Veltros were manufactured, leaving a promising airplane clearly a victim of a war that refused to stand still and wait for it.

Specifications for the MC.205V

Length: 29ft 1in
Wingspan: 34ft 9in
Height: 10ft 0in

Wing area: 181 sq ft
Empty weight: 5,691lb
Maximum speed: 399mph at 23,620ft
Maximum range: 645 miles
Service ceiling: 36,090ft
Rate of climb: 3,700ft/min

Surviving Examples

MC.205V
'MM9345' – Italian Air Force Museum
'MM9327' – Museo Nationale della Scienza e della Tecnica, Milan

Reggiane Re.2000 Falco I

Most accusations of having copied another's fighter design, such as the amazing suggestion that the Japanese Zero was a copy of the Hughes Racer(!), have been found to be more imagination that logic. Not so for the Italian Reggiane 2000, whose similarities to the American Seversky P-35 are hard to overlook. The major difference was the installation of a 1,000hp Piaggio radial engine in the Reggiane 2000.

Tests showed the 2000 to be superior to the MC.200 in most respects, and in one series of tests, the Italian fighter bested a Bf 109 in simulated dog fighting, even when the latter was flown by German pilots. But it was determined that it had several important deficiencies, including some structural weaknesses and badly located fuel tanks. The Macchi was thus selected for production by the Italian Air Ministry, while the Reggiane was slated for export. Sixty were bought by the Swedish Flygvapnet in 1940, remaining in service into 1945.

The same year, Hungary ordered some and then produced more with 1,000hp Gnome-Rhone, engines, operating them on the Eastern Front. The Italian Navy then showed interest in a version modified for carrier use with strengthened landing gear. Total production the Re.2000 was limited to 170 airplanes, as it was quickly replaced on the assembly lines by the improved Re.2001 Falco II.

Specifications of the Re.2000

Length: 26ft 6in
Wingspan: 36ft 1in
Height: 10ft 6in
Wing area: 220 sq ft
Empty weight: 4,585lb
Maximum speed: 329mph at 16,400ft

Maximum range: 520 miles
Service ceiling: 36,745ft
Rate of climb: 3,175 ft/min

Surviving Example

Re.2000
(J20) Fv 2340 – Flygvapnetmuseum, Linkoping, Sweden

Reggiane Re.2002 Ariete (Ram)

This follow-on to the limited-production Alfa Romeo V-12-powered Re.2001, resembled the earlier Re.2000/P-35 in that it used a Piaggio 14-cylinder radial engine. This was chosen because the 2002 was meant for the low-altitude fighter-bomber role where the more durable radial engine shone, and also because the V-12 engines were not expected to be available in sufficient numbers. Compared with the Re.2001, it was slightly slower, had a reduced rate of climb, lower ceiling, but a somewhat greater range. Armament was the same: two .30 cal. and two .50 cal. machine guns, while the latter could carry up to 1,400lb of bombs.

It was first assigned to squadrons in 1942, which used them in the defense of the Allied invasion of Sicily, during which most of the Re.2002s were destroyed. No more than 50 were built, most of which were used by units that fought on the Axis side after the Italian Government surrendered to the Allies.

Direct developments included the Re.2003 reconnaissance bomber which failed to advance beyond prototype stage, and the Re.2004 which would have been powered by a 1,250hp Isotta Fraschini X-24 engine, but its development was stopped by the Armistice. The final Reggiane Re.2005 was a throwback to the Re.2001, with a 1,475hp Fiat-built DB 605 engine, which might have become one of the best of all the Italian fighters, except that fewer than 50 went into squadron operations before the Armistice.

Specifications for the Re.2002

Length: 26ft 10in
Wingspan: 36ft 1in
Height: 10ft 4in
Wing area: 220 sq ft
Empty weight: 5,270lb
Maximum speed: 329mph at 18,050ft
Maximum range: 685 miles at 19,685ft
Service ceiling: 34,450ft
Rate of climb: 2,600 ft/min

Surviving Examples

Re.2002
DV+BI – Musee de la Resistance du Centre, Limoges, France

Chapter Thirteen

Japan

Nakajima Ki.27 'Nate'

In the late 1930s Japan was finally beginning to emerge from the era of the open-cockpit, fabric-covered biplane with fixed landing gear, into the modern day. And while its first efforts produced much higher performance airplanes, their reliance on lightweight structures aimed at superior maneuverability brought with it insufficient resistance to battle damage. When thrown into battle against Soviet fighters of the late 1930s, they first did well, then suffered in comparison with even slightly more modern enemy designs.

The first of the airplanes to employ more modern ideas was the Ki.27, the first Japanese fighter to be a monoplane and to have a full cockpit canopy. The prototype flew in October 1936, almost a year after the Hawker Hurricane and more than a year after the Messerschmitt Bf 109. The Ki.27s empty weight of under 2,500lb was little more than half that of those airplanes, thanks to unusually light construction. The aim was an airplane having exceptional maneuverability.

Production was begun in 1937, and the first airplanes were in action in 1938 against Soviet I-15s in Manchuria. By the spring of 1939, hundreds were in combat, performing well against their opposition until the I-15s were replaced by more powerful Polikarpov I-16s. It was only the ability to turn tightly that enabled them to hold their own in dogfights.

The original Ki.27 began to be replaced by the cleaned-up Ki.27bis in 1939, which was used extensively in China and throughout south-east Asia. A Ki.27-KAI was considered, but with newer airplanes coming along, including Nakajima's Ki.43 'Oscar', the idea was dropped after only three were built. When the production run ended in 1940, the total manufactured was 3,386, some of which were operated by the Japanese-controlled Manchurian Air Force.

Specifications of the Ki.27

Length: 24ft 9in
Wingspan: 37ft 2in
Height: 9ft 2in
Wing area: 200 sq ft
Empty weight: 2,447lb
Maximum speed: 286mph at 16,400ft
Maximum range: 389 miles
Service ceiling: 39,900 ft
Rate of climb: 2,950 ft

Surviving Example

Ki-27
Tachiarai Peace Memorial Museum

Nakajima Ki.43 Hayabusa (Peregrine Falcon) 'Oscar'

The logical next step for Nakajima after the Ki.27 'Nate' was an airplane with more power, heavier armament and retractable landing gear. It continued the philosophy of favoring maneuverability over survivability, for which Japan paid an increasingly high price as the war progressed.

The Ki.43 'Oscar' retained its predecessor's lightweight structure, but initially suffered from surprisingly poor maneuverability and heavy controls. To solve this, engineers developed 'maneuvering' or 'combat' flaps which extended beyond the trailing edge of the wing and by increasing their area, reduced the turn radius. The result was one of the most nimble fighters of the Pacific war.

The first production model of the Ki.43 was the -1A, powered by the 950hp Ha.25 radial engine and having a top speed of just over 300mph. As it didn't go into production until March 1941, it was obsolescent and soon was replaced by the -1B and the -1C, which had no more than two .50 cal. machine guns. When the United States entered the war in late 1941, few 'Oscars' were with front-line units. While they could out-maneuver even the latest American fighters, their inability to survive more than minor battle damage made them easy prey.

Specifications of the Ki.43-IIB

Length: 29ft 3in
Wingspan: 37ft 7in
Height: 10ft 2in
Wing area: 232 sq ft
Empty weight: 3,812lb
Maximum speed: 320mph at 19,680ft
Maximum range: 1,865 miles with external fuel

Service ceiling: 36,800ft
Rate of climb: 5:49 to 16,400ft

Surviving Examples

Ki.43-Ib
Japan 62387 – US National Air & Space Museum
c/n 750 – Flying Heritage Collection
Tillamook (Oregon) Air Museum

Ki.43-II
H 45 – Museum Pusat

Ki.43-IIB
c/n 6430 and 15267 – Boeing Museum of Flight (on loan from NASM)

Kawasaki Ki.45 Toryu (Dragon Killer) 'Nick'

Heavy, long-range, twin-engined fighters were occupying the time of war planners in many countries in the late 1930s, with Japan's entry into this new arena being the Ki.45 'Nick'. Designed as the Ki.38 in 1937, it emerged from extensive redesign to become a production airplane in 1941.

The original Nakajima Ha.20B radial engines failed to deliver even their promised 820hp, and not even Kawasaki's attempt to redesign the engine and to use contra-rotating propellers made much difference. It was finally replaced by the 1,000hp Ha.25 in the Ki.45-I, the prototype of which flew in July 1940, production not starting until September 1941.

One of the best of the Japanese night fighters, 'Nick' was produced in quantity, almost 1,700 coming off the assembly lines in two large factories. The first of scores of major raids by B-29s then operating from bases in China was met by Ki.45s, whose pilots claimed seven destroyed.

As an improvement on the Ki.45-Ic, Kawasaki proceeded to build the first of the Ki.45-II, a single-seat fighter designated the Ki.96, and powered by two Mitsubishi Ha.112 engines rated at 1,500hp. Top speed and rate of climb showed major increases over the Ki.45, but official support was lacking and only a prototype was built. Many components of it were used in the Ki.102 'Randy', which had a 57mm cannon, a single .50 cal. machine gun and a capacity of 1,100lb of bombs. Only two were produced, due to the extent of the damage done to the factory by 20th US Air Force B-29s.

Specifications of the Ki.45-KAIc

Length: 36ft 1in
Wingspan: 49ft 5in
Height: 12ft 2in
Wing area: 344 sq ft
Empty weight: 8,818lb
Maximum speed: 340mph at 22,965ft
Maximum range: 932 miles
Service ceiling: 32,810ft
Rate of climb: 2,300 ft/min

Surviving Example

Ki.45 KAI
USAAF FE-701 – US National Air & Space Museum

It had a forward-firing fixed armament of a single 20mm cannon and two .50 cal. machine guns, plus a single flexible .30 cal. machine gun for the rear-facing backseat observer. There were shackles under the wing center sections for a pair of 550lb bombs A year later, the Ki.45-Ic went into production with two 1,100hp Ha.102 engines. It followed the Ki.45-Ib, which was armed with a variety of machine guns and cannon up to 75mm.

The Ki.45c and Ki.45d were the first to be developed for night fighting, many of them mounting two 20mm cannon installed on top of the fuselage and just behind the pilot and pointing upward at 30 degrees. These were used to attack, from underneath, the increasingly large formations of American bombers assaulting the Japanese homeland. The unusual idea was considered so successful that it was soon adopted by the German Luftwaffe.

Kawasaki Ki.61 Hien (Swallow) 'Tony'

While all the other major aerial combatants relied to a great extent on fighters powered by liquid-cooled V-12 engines, the only such design produced in Japan was less than a great success until a version powered by an air-cooled radial engine was developed. The aerodynamic advantages of the smaller V-12 were out-weighed by the lack of reliability of Japan's sole production V-12.

The first of the in-line fighters was the Kawasaki Ki.60, which used a license-built German Daimler-Benz DB 601A rated at 1,100hp. Unfortunately, it ran into the resistance of pilots to the inevitable increases in take-off and landing distances and reduced maneuverability due to its higher wing-loading. Plans for production were cancelled in late 1941 after only three airplanes had been built.

Its replacement, the Ki.61, was already under construction, the first one flying at the same time the Ki.60 was dropped from long-range planning. The first to be delivered with an 1,175hp Japanese-built version of the DB (called the 601 Kawasaki Ha.40) to an operational unit arrived in August 1942, with production increasing to 100 per month by July 1944. At first, 'Tonys' carried two .50 cal. machine guns in the nose and two .30 cal. machine guns in the wings, the latter soon replaced by the larger type. To these was added a single 20mm German cannon until the ability of the maker to supply the guns dried up.

While the Ki.61 was considered nearly the equal of the US Army and Navy fighters in the Pacific, it suffered by being difficult to service in the crude conditions of island warfare, and the engines lacked mechanical reliability. With dependable examples of the Ha.40 engine in short supply, plans were made to adopt the new 1,500hp Kawasaki Ha.140. The new engine, however, wa experiencing its own troubles, and the need to correct structural weakness in the new Ki.61-II-KAI airframe demanded a major redesign.

Few of the follow-on version had been completed due to increasing engine limitations, when a raid by a large force of B-29s ended the program. Plans to produce a version with a semi-bubble canopy were scrapped in favor of re-equipping with a radial engine that would offer greater reliability. It was designated the Ki.100.

Specifications of the Ki.61

Length: 27ft 10in
Wingspan: 34ft 6in
Height: 9ft 10in
Wing area: 174 sq ft
Empty weight: 5,800 lb
Maximum speed: 348 mph
Maximum range: 360 miles
Rate of climb: 3,300 ft/min

Surviving Examples

Ki.61
c/n 379 – Fantasy of Flight

Ki.61-IIKai
c/n 5070 – Kamikaze Memorial Museum

Nakajima Ki.84 Hayate (Gale) 'Frank'

Japan's best all-around fighter-bomber was the culmination of the gradual shift in design philosophy from emphasizing maneuverability and rate of climb to the detriment of speed and durability, to the thinking of its enemies who stressed speed, firepower and resistance to battle damage. Had the change in thinking at the highest level of command been made sooner, the Allies would no doubt have had a more difficult fight on their hands.

The change can be traced back to the late 1930s, when the design of the Ki.43 'Oscar' was accompanied by the initial work that produced the Nakajima Ki.44 'Tojo'. While the 'Oscar' was typically light and flimsy, the 'Tojo', which first flew in 1940, was substantially heavier and more powerful. Reticence on the part of fighter pilots accustomed to low take-off and landing speeds, and excellent maneuverability, was eventually replaced by acceptance

of the positive qualities of the more modern airplane. Production exceeded 1,200 and was ended only when the Ki.44 was replaced by an even heavier and sturdier Ki.84.

In 1944 Japan introduced its most Western of fighters, with a 1,900hp Nakajima Ha.45 radial engine, whose effectiveness was nevertheless compromised by mechanical shortcomings. Other problems involved the hydraulic system and the landing gear. Despite all this, the airplane was easily the best Japanese air defense weapon, being used in all theaters of war. Additionally, it performed well as a dive bomber.

Late in its production, the increasing shortage of modern aluminum alloys led to efforts to replace them first with wood (Ki.106) and then with steel (Ki.113). Increases in weight due to the use of such less-than-ideal materials, cut into the otherwise excellent performance. To counter this set-back, the Ki.84-III was planned with a 2,000hp engine, but the war ended before any could be built.

This was the end of the line for a family of fighters that had begun with the nimble Ki.43. The game had changed, and Japan was unable to meet the best of the Allied fighters on even terms, due in part to the drop in the quality of workmanship in the factories that were an increasingly frequent target of bombing raids.

Specifications for the Ki.84

Length: 32ft 7in
Wingspan: 36ft 10in
Height: 11ft 1in
Wing area: 226 sq ft
Empty weight: 5,864lb

Maximum speed: 388mph at 19,680ft
Maximum range: 1,815 miles at 173mph
Service ceiling: 34,450ft
Rate of climb: 5:54 to 16,400ft

Surviving Example

Ki.84
c/n 1446 – Kamikaze Memorial Museum, Kagoshima

Kawasaki Ki.100 'Tony'

The Ki.61 was Japan's only fighter powered by an inverted V-12 engine, starting out with German DB 601s and soon switching to the Japanese version, called the Kawasaki Ha.40. The supply of engines dwindled, leaving more than 250 engineless airframes parked at the factory. With air attacks battering the production facilities, the need for these airplanes to be completed necessitated extreme measures.

Bolting a large radial engine to the front of an airplane designed for something very different probably should have produced sub-standard performance and some odd flying characteristics. In this case, the exact opposite resulted, with the quick modification resulted in a much better airplane than the original Ki.61 'Tony'. Armament consisted of two .50 cal. machine guns and two 20mm cannon, by now the fairly standard equipment for Japanese fighters.

Two hundred and fifty were converted between March and May 1945, at which time production of the Ki.Ib began. Eighty-eight had been constructed by late July 1945, when bombing raids

Maximum speed: 367mph at 32,800ft
Maximum range: 1,243 miles
Service ceiling: 35,000ft
Rate of climb: 6:42 to 16,400ft

Surviving Example

Ki.100
c/n 16336 – RAF Museum (Hendon)

Mitsubishi A6M Zero-Sen 'Zeke'

did extensive damage to the factory. Another 35 were built in the following two weeks before the war ended. A factory-built Ki.100 differed from a modified 'Tony' by having a bubble canopy instead of the original type which was faired into the turtledeck.

An improved version – Ki.100-II – got as far as prototype form, when it was determined that the new turbo-supercharger's weight reduced, rather than improved performance.

Specifications of the Ki.100

Length: 28ft 11in
Wingspan: 39ft 4in
Height: 12ft 4in
Wing area: 215 sq ft
Empty weight: 5,952lb

The Zero fighter must be rated as one of the great surprises of World War Two, having been developed by a nation generally thought to be far behind the US, Great Britain and Germany in the science and technology of flight. Moreover, it was the first naval fighter to outperform land-based fighters, and the first Japanese fighter with a closed cockpit and retractable landing gear. However, in order to achieve its maneuverability and rate of climb, the design lacked structural rigidity, armor plate and self-sealing fuel tanks, all of which would prove to be major handicaps.

The prototype of the A6M1 flew in April 1939, and could reach 300mph on the power of a 780hp radial engine. This marked it as a significant advance on its immediate predecessor, the A5M4 'Claude'. After just two prototypes were built, the A6M1 was replaced by the A6M2, which had a 925hp engine and could attain 332mph, which was faster than the Japanese Air Force's latest fighter, the Ki.43 'Oscar', then at the same stage of development.

Such was the urgency of the war's demands that 15 pre-production A6M2s were rushed to China, where they proved themselves to be far superior to all of China's outdated fighters.

More than 400 of this model were available to Japan's carrier forces by the time of the Pearl Harbor attack in December 1941. This was the United States' first direct experience with the Zero, which showed its superior speed and maneuverability to the US Navy's Grumman F4F Wildcats and Brewster F2A Buffaloes and the Army's Curtiss P-40s.

The A6M3 had flown six months before, with an 1,130hp engine and aerodynamic changes which improved its performance across the board. It was soon seen in quantity in every area where Japan was fighting, but was starting to lose its position as the top fighter of the Pacific war as it encountered much more modern P-38 Lightnings, F4U Corsairs and P-51 Mustangs. Its inability to survive the heavier firepower of American fighters was becoming an increasingly serious handicap.

With newer designs not yet ready to replace the Zero in squadron service, it fell to Mitsubishi to improve both its performance and durability. The A6M5 was a somewhat improved version, the first of which entered combat in the spring of 1944 and soon became the most common model of the Zero. It was still unable to keep pace with the deliveries of faster and much more heavily armored fighters it was meeting at every turn.

The A6M8c was the final production version, and had a 1,560hp Mitsubishi engine equipped with water-methanol injection, along with heavier armament of two 20mm cannon and three .50 cal. machine guns, plus two air-to-air rockets under either wing. As production continued, airplanes appeared with more armor and self-sealing fuel tanks which reduced in-flight fires. Top speed finally exceeded 350mph. While still very much a naval airplane, its use was limited to land air bases as the Japanese carrier force was being all but eliminated in major sea battles.

The Zero's replacement was to have been the Mitsubishi A7M series Reppu (Hurricane), or 'Sam' in the Allied system of names. It was aerodynamically cleaned up and had a 2,200hp 18-cylinder radial engine, yet a top speed of only 390mph at 21,000ft. Plans for large-scale production ran afoul of mass American bombing raids and Mother Nature, who produced a large earthquake that seriously reduced production. More heavy raids ended any hopes of producing enough fighters to make a difference.

In total, the Zero exceeded all other types of Japanese World War Two fighters, with just over 10,000 built. It was unquestionably that nation's most significant military airplane.

Specifications of the A6M3, Model 32

Length: 29ft 9in
Wingspan: 36ft 1in
Height: 11ft 6in
Wing area: 232 sq ft
Empty weight: 3,985lb
Maximum speed: 338mph at 19,685ft
Maximum range: 1,500 miles
Service ceiling: 36,250ft
Rate of climb: 4,500ft/min

Surviving Examples

A6M2
c/n 5784 – Australian War Museum
c/n 51553 – National Museum of the US Air Force
Fargo, N.D.

A6M2b
c/n 5450 – National Naval Aviation Museum

A6M3
Japan Y2-128 – Aichi Air & Space Museum
c/n 3844 – Auckland Institute and Museum, New Zealand
c/n 3318 – Evergreen Air Museum
c/n 3852 – Flying Heritage Collection

A6M5
Japan 61-131 – US National Air & Space Museum
c/n 1303 – Flying Heritage Collection

Japan 5357 – Planes of Fame
c/n 4241 – Yasukuni Shrine, Tokyo
m/s 30-1153 – Museum Pusat Tri-An
c/n 4400 – Air Heritage Collection, Hamamatsu
c/n 4708 – Mitsubishi Heavy Industries

A6M5a
c/n 4685 – Air Heritage Collection, Hamamatsu
c/n 4708 – Mitsubishi Heavy Industries

A6M5c
m/s 22383 – Japan Self Defense Force Museum, Kanoya

A6M7
Japan B118 – Kuri Marine Museum
Japan E-143 – US National Air & Space Museum

Nakajima J1N1 Gekko (Moonlight) 'Irving'

The Gekko had a very confused start in life. It began as a design for a long-range, twin-engined escort fighter, then evolved into a combination long-range escort, night intruder and high-speed reconnaissance airplane. The first examples were ordered as solely a reconnaissance airplane, but when the need for night fighters emerged, it changed its stripes once again.

The Japanese Navy first showed interest in a modern long-range airplane as far back as 1938 when it asked manufacturers to create a large, multi-place airplane that could fly far and still meet small, single-engined fighters on even terms: a combination beyond any known airplane's ability to meet. The result was an airplane too large and too heavy to have the desired maneuverability, even though it was to have been equipped with all the latest high-lift devices, including leading edge slots, large flaps and opposite-rotating propellers to reduce the effects of torque.

The prototype J1N1 flew in May 1941, with a novel array of guns: fixed, forward-firing 20mm cannon and two .30 cal. machine guns, plus rear-firing pairs of .30 cal. machine guns contained in remote-controlled barbettes. The latter proved entirely too complicated and were soon removed. Additionally, severe aileron flutter and ineffectiveness could not be corrected and the escort fighter was rejected.

As a reconnaissance airplane, the J1N1-C, powered with 1,130hp 14-cylinder radial engines, entered the war in early 1943 in the Solomon Islands, where the American island-hopping program was beginning. With B-17 and B-24 operations interfering seriously

with the Japanese Army air forces, the need for a night fighter reemerged, as did a new technique for installing guns. Two fixed 20mm cannon were mounted atop the J1N1-C, aimed forward and 30 degrees upward, while two more were in the bottom, firing 30 degrees rearward. Bomber pilots were unprepared for being shot at by enemy airplanes flying directly above or below them, and losses occurred until this novel means of attack had been studied, and defensive maneuvers developed.

A final purpose-built night fighter – the J1N1-S – had a two-gun top turret, but retained the fixed dorsal and ventral guns. This proved an effective combat airplane until the appearance of faster, higher-flying B-29s carrying a more advanced fire control system. Total production amounted to just 480, including prototypes. The plan was to replace the Gekko with Nakajima's J5N1 Tenrai.

Specifications of the J1N1-S

Length: 40ft 0in
Wingspan: 55ft 9in
Height: 13ft 2in
Wing area: 431 sq ft
Empty weight: 10,697lb
Maximum speed: 315mph at 19,030ft
Maximum range: 1,500 miles
Service ceiling: 30,590ft
Rate of climb: 5:01 to 9,800ft

Surviving Example

J1N1-S
c/n 7334 – US National Air & Space Museum

Mitsubishi J2M Raiden (Thunderbolt) 'Jack'

With the Zero having raised Japan's stature among countries operating effective fighters, its day was passing. Mitsubishi then headed in another direction, replacing its reliance on lightly-built, unprotected airplanes whose outstanding maneuverability was their primary defense, with more modern, solidly-built airplanes that used speed and rate of climb in an effort to regain that nation's once superior position. The J2M 'Jack' was more in line with worldwide practice.

The prototype 'Jack' – the J2M1 – flew in March 1942, but suffered from a series of drawbacks, including speed and rate of climb that failed to meet government requirements. It was soon followed by the J2M2 with a larger Mitsubishi MK4R Kasai 1,800hp engine turning a four-bladed propeller. Testing and then production were slowed by a series of accidents in which airplanes came apart for no immediately apparent reason. Fixes were implemented, but only reduced the rate of catastrophic accidents.

Finally, a new canopy offering improved visibility became standard, but not until the J2M6 went into production in June 1944. Most Raiden pilots were seriously handicapped by the lack of all-around vision.

By the time the first of the J2M2s were going into service, they were being replaced on the assembly line by the J2M3. Armament was gradually increased, with the J2M3 having four 20mm cannon in the wings. To improve the airplane, which had been meant from the beginning as an interceptor, its high-altitude performance was enhanced by installation of a turbo-supercharger. The J2M4, which first flew in August 1944, had the imposing armament of six 20mm cannon, but experienced repeated problems with its supercharger and never went into production.

Even before the first one had flown, the J2M5 was on the assembly line. Despite having its guns reduced to just two cannon, its top speed of 380mph made it the best of the Raiden versions against the high-flying B-29 formations. The engine builder, however, was unable to meet the demand and fewer than 50 J2M5 were built and delivered.

'Jack' made its combat debut in September 1944, in the battle of the Mariana Islands and fared well against individual American fighters, but was badly outnumbered and suffered accordingly. They struggled to cope with the ever-larger formations of B-29s that dumped thousands of tons of bombs on Japanese cities in the closing months of the war. Even if there had been 500 of them flown by well-trained pilots, the war still would have ended in the same way.

Specifications of the J2M3 Raiden 21

Length: 31ft 10in
Wingspan: 35ft 5in
Height: 12ft 8in
Wing area: 216 sq ft
Empty weight: 5,423lb
Maximum speed: 371mph at 19,360ft
Maximum range: 655 miles at 265mph at 19,685ft with 31-gallon drop tank
Service ceiling: 38,385ft
Rate of climb: 3,200 ft/min

Surviving Example

J2M3
Japan 91-101 – Planes of Fame

Nakajima J5N1 Tenrai (Heavenly Thunder)

As Japan's ability to design modern, high-performance airplanes improved, its capacity for quantity production of such machines decreased due to American capture of island bases which made possible more and larger bombing raids, thus rendering one project after another impotent. At the same time, its primary enemy, the US Army Air Forces, was enjoying a flood of superior combat airplanes, well trained pilots to fly them and a sophisticated supply system equal to the task of supporting a rapidly expanding offensive force.

The J5N1 was one of those airplanes that might have made a difference, had it not been suffering from production problems and the inability of the defense forces to protect its hard-pressed factories. The first prototype of this promising twin-engined fighter flew in March 1944, powered by two 2,000hp Nakajima Homare 18-cylinder engines. Its top speed and rate of climb, combined with the heavy armament of two 30mm cannon and two 20mm cannon, should have made it a serious threat to the fast, high-flying B-29s which would soon appear in great numbers over the Japanese homeland.

Progress was impeded by the failure of the engines to produce their promised power, and by a steady increase in the weight of the airframe as the need to reverse the long-standing policy of giving low priority to armor protection led to a build-up of weight and a drop in performance. It became increasingly apparent that only major changes would correct the problems.

When most of the prototypes were lost to accidents or air attacks, the Naval Air Force decided the time needed to rectify the Tenrai's shortcomings was unacceptable, and the program was cancelled.

Specifications of the J5N1

Length: 37ft 9in
Wingspan: 47ft 7in
Height: 11ft 6in
Wing area: 344 sq ft
Empty weight: 11,453lb
Maximum speed: 386mph at 20,000ft
Maximum range: 575 miles
Service ceiling: 35,430ft
Rate of climb: 8:00 to 19,700ft

Surviving Example

J5N1
US National Air & Space Museum (pieces)

Kyushu J7W1 Shinden (Magnificent Lightning)

Few designs for radical fighters progressed beyond the drawing board during or immediately preceding World War Two, even though many had the potential for considerably better performance than the conventional fighters being turned out by the tens of thousands. Of these, only three canard (tail-first) designs were built by the major combatants: the Italian S.A.I. SS.4 (one built), the American Curtiss XP-55 Ascender (three prototypes) and the Japanese Kyushu J7W1, of which just two were built and flown. None entered production.

The Shinden dated back to a trio of gliders tested in late 1943 with considerable success. Even before the tests had been completed, plans for the construction of the prototype J7W1 and for its quantity production were set in motion. Prototype construction began in June 1944, with the first of two flying on 3 August 1945. A production rate of 150 per month was forecast for late 1946, by which time the war would have been over for more than a year. It was powered by a 2,100hp Mitsubishi Ha.43-42 18-cylinder, air-cooled radial engine.

The Shinden appears to have been a good airplane, with no more faults than any other new design. The tail-first arrangement was expected to produce advantages of reduced drag, superior pilot visibility and no need for its four 30mm cannon to have the interruptor mechanism required for guns firing through a propeller arc. But, like the Italian and American experiments, it was not able to convince the cautious ruling powers that such an adventurous scheme was worth the risks.

Specifications of the J7W1

Length: 30ft 5in
Wingspan: 36ft 6in
Height: 12ft 11in
Wing area: 221 sq ft
Empty weight: 7,640lb
Maximum speed: 466mph at 28,540ft estimated
Maximum range: 528 miles estimated
Service ceiling: 39,000ft estimated
Rate of climb: 2,450 ft/min

Surviving Examples

J7W1
USAAF FE-326 – US National Air & Space Museum

Mitsubishi J8M Shusui (Shining Blade)

Japan desperately needed a high-performance interceptor to provide point defense for especially vital factories and other basic manufacturing facilities, which were the targets of increasingly large formations of well-armed American heavy bombers. Lacking anything of their own, they turned to Axis partner Germany, which was making great progress with its Messerschmitt Me 163 rocket-powered interceptor. For a price, Germany agreed to cooperate with the Japanese Navy, and shipped a sample Me 163 and all the information required to place it into large-scale production. It looked like a solution just might be at hand.

At this point, the US Navy stepped in, sinking the submarine which was on its way to deliver the rocket plane and engineering materials, and leaving the Japanese with just one German rocket motor and scattered bits of data. Japanese Navy engineers did their best to duplicate the Komet, starting with an unpowered version called the MXY8 to train pilots in some of the tail-less airplane's flight characteristics. At least 50 of the gliders were built, with some being used by the Army Air Force, whose interest was growing and would soon lead to definite plans to have the tailless interceptor produced in quantity.

The first glider was flown in November 1944, while the German rocket motor was being adapted for Japanese production methods. The first powered J8M1 was flown from the Yokosuka Naval Base on 7 July 1945. After a normal take off and climb to 1,300 feet, the motor suddenly stopped and the prototype crashed, killing the test pilot. The cause of the accident was never pinned down, but several modifications were suggested, including the removal of one of the two 30mm cannon to provide space for additional fuel.

Before a second airplane could be completed and tested, the war ended. That single flight, brief as it may have been, may well have been the historic final flight of any solely rocket-powered fighter.

Specifications of the J8M1

Length: 9ft 2in
Wingspan: 31ft 2in
Height: 8ft 10in
Wing area: 191 sq ft
Empty weight: 3,186lb
Maximum speed: 497mph at 32,800ft estimated
Maximum duration: 5.5 minutes under power estimated
Service ceiling: never determined
Rate of climb: 9,000+ft/min estimated

Surviving Examples

J8M1
Japan 403 – Planes of Fame
Mitsubishi Heavy Industries

Kawanishi N1K1 Kyofu (Mighty Wind) 'Rex'

'Rex' was one-of-a-kind in the annals of military aviation: a floatplane fighter with such excellent performance that it led directly to a major land-based fighter. It had the sleek lines and powerful look of a serious competitor in one of the Schneider Trophy Races of the early 1930s.

The N1K1 was intended to be used by in support of advancing ground forces in areas lacking even the most rudimentary of landing fields. By the time it was being delivered to air force units, the Japanese Army had ceased its expansion efforts and was in retreat on many fronts, and so the special qualities of the N1K1 were no longer needed.

The basic idea of a high-performance floatplane fighter was unique to the Japanese, and was carried out exceptionally well in this seaplane. Its advanced streamlining, the considerable power of its 14-cylinder radial engine, surprisingly strong structure and heavy armament of two .30 cal. machine guns and two 20mm cannon resulted in performance surprisingly close to that of comparable land-based fighters.

The first test flight of the prototype was in May 1942, just a few months after the US entered the war with the likes of Curtiss P-40s and Grumman F4Fs. But by the time the first 'Rex' arrived at operational units in July changes were being felt, and its superiority was vanishing. As a result, only 89 were delivered in almost a year of production.

With land-based and carrier-based naval fighters taking over responsibilities, the 'Rex' had its huge main float and two smaller wingtip floats replaced by wheeled landing gear to become the N1K1-J 'George'. It is no doubt due to its quick and early retirement that any 'Rex' have survived.

Empty weight: 6,065lb
Maximum speed: 304mph at 18,700ft
Maximum range: 1,035 miles
Service ceiling: 34,645ft
Rate of climb: 5:32 to 16,500ft

Surviving Examples

N1K1
c/n 562 – Admiral Nimitz Museum
c/n 565 – NAS Willow Grove, Pa.

Specifications of the N1K1

Length: 34ft 9in
Wingspan: 39ft 5in
Height: 15ft 7in
Wing area: 253 sq ft

Kawanishi N1K2-J Shiden (Violet Lightning) 'George'

Even before the first 'Rex' had flown, the manufacturer had seen the need and the opportunity to develop a land-based fighter with most of its good features and no more of its drawbacks than could be avoided. The resultant N1K1-J 'George' ranks as probably the best all-around, mass-produced, single-seat Japanese fighter of the war.

The original 'George' far surpassed contemporary Japanese fighters in its speed, firepower and resistance to damage, while retaining the beloved maneuverability of the Zero and its predecessors. But it was rushed into production before its bugs could be ironed out, with a 2,000hp 18-cylinder radial engine that should have been under development rather than in production. Combining an unproven airframe and an unproven engine guaranteed problems that would take time to perfect, just as time was beginning to run out.

The first test flight of the prototype was in the early summer of 1943 and revealed serious problems with its 2,000hp Nakajima Homare 14-cylinder radial engine which were to retard development of the fighter throughout its service life. The airplane was rushed into production, requiring numerous changes and slowing progress even more. Yet the performance was outstanding, and there was no thought of cancelling it.

Just over 1,000 were built before December 1943, when highly effective bombing raids stopped production. This airplane brought the Japanese Naval Air Service into the modern age, its four 20mm cannon and excellent maneuverability making it clearly superior to the F6F Hellcat. It was soon to face the F4U Corsair and P-51D Mustang, which were to prove more difficult opponents.

The Shiden was intended mainly to counter the increasingly large formations of B-29 Superfortress heavy bombers that were pouring large bomb loads on the homeland. This called for a major improvement on the initial production version, which had continued problems with engines and landing gears. The result was the N1K2-J Shiden-Kai. By lowering the wing from the low-mid position to a more conventional low wing, the complicated retraction method for the long landing gear was eliminated. The entire airframe was simplified with an eye towards quicker construction. The troublesome engine remained the same, as did the armament of four 20mm cannon.

Eight prototypes were flying by the early summer of 1944, but quantity production was delayed until March 1945 due to bombing-induced shortages of engines, specialized construction

Maximum speed: 362mph at 10,000ft
Maximum range: 1,450 miles
Service ceiling: 35,300ft
Rate of climb: 2,515 ft/min

Surviving Examples

N1K2-Ja
Japan 343-35 – National Museum of the US Air Force
c/n 5341 – US National Air & Space Museum
c/n 5128 – National Naval Aviation Museum

materials and major sub-assemblies. While seven factories were brought into the operation, only 425 airplanes were completed, far too few to reduce the effectiveness of mass raids by B-29s. Several advanced versions were under consideration, including the N1K5-J with a 2,200hp Mitsubishi engine, the sole prototype of which was destroyed in a raid.

Specifications of the N1K2-J

Length: 30ft 8in
Wingspan: 39ft 4in
Height: 13ft 0in
Wing area: 253 sq ft
Empty weight: 5,890lb

Nakajima Kikka (Orange Blossom)

If not for government indifference, Japan might have developed turbojet and turboprop engines before any other country, having begun studies as early as 1920. As it turned out, the Japanese trailed Germany, Britain, the United States and Italy, all of which flew jet-propelled airplanes before the end of World War Two. Illustrative of the chaos existing in Japan in the summer of 1945, neither the designation nor even the name of the manufacturer can be determined with any confidence.

The first thinking in the jet direction was by Admiral Hanajima and was based on French supercharger developments. It wasn't until news of European turbojet designs being patented in the late 1930s that he delved deeper into the technology of both turbines and rocket motors, finally attracting official support only when the belated news that Japan's Axis ally had tested its first jet-powered airplanes in 1939.

Japan's first jet engine – the Ne 10 – was run initially in 1943 and produced considerably less power than expected. By then, not only Germany but Great Britain and the USA had flown pre-production airplanes on turbojet power and were moving rapidly toward fighters with far greater speed than anything that had preceded them.

Realizing it was far behind the other nations, Japan requested help from its ally, Nazi Germany. In 1944, when the war in the Pacific had swung decisively in favor of the Allies, Germany finally agreed to send assistance by licensing Japan to build both the Me 262 jet fighter and the Me 163 rocket fighter. As Japan needed considerable technical assistance in the form of construction drawings and samples of specialized hardware, Germany shipped engine blueprints by submarine, accompanied by a Japanese Navy officer.

The portion of the trip that had begun in April 1944, had gotten no further than Singapore by July at which time the Commander flew on to Tokyo with a limited quantity of paperwork. The remainder of the materiel continued on by submarine until the US Navy ended the journey by sinking it. The Japanese were left with nothing more than a few pieces of paper.

Desperate by this time, they modified their original Ne 10 into the much better Ne 12, of which several were built. Installation of two Ne 12 was authorized in September but construction was slowed by a severe shortage of the high-temperature metals vital to jet engines. The Kikka bore a superficial resemblance to the Me 262, but was smaller and less powerful, with such a high fuel consumption that its range was estimated at no more than 100 miles.

Unknown to the world, Japan had tested the prototype of its Mitsubishi J8M copy of the Me 163 Komet rocket-powered interceptor. A few seconds after take-off, it crashed and killed its test pilot, further discouraging those who sensed the impending end.

The first Kikka was completed with turbojet engines developed from the BMW 003 which was rated at more than 1,000lb of thrust, and its engines were run at the end of June 1945. There was obviously little time left, as the word had been passed to the Allies that the Japanese government was considering an honorable surrender, rather than the absolute victory demanded by the Allies.

Finally, on the day after the world's first atomic bomb had been dropped on Hiroshima, the first test flight of a Kikka was made successfully. Another four days passed and a second flight was readied, this time with high officials present. Due to the pilot's misinterpretation of the impact of booster rockets stopping, it skidded into Tokyo Bay.

The all-out sprint to the finish line had ended short of the wire. Japan surrendered and dozens of unfinished Kikka airframes that were found in the factory became a monument to an impossible task.

Specifications of the Kikka

Length: 26ft 8in
Wingspan: 32ft 10in
Height: 9ft 9in
Wing area: 142 sq ft
Empty weight: 5,070lb
Maximum speed: 433mph estimated
Maximum range: 586 miles estimated
Service ceiling: 39,370ft estimated
Rate of climb: 1,235ft/min estimated

Surviving Example

Kikka
Unknown m/s – US National Air & Space Museum

Extinct World War Two Types

Of more than 200 basic types of fighters built in connection with World War Two, some 95 types have survived, while another 120+ have become extinct. Almost half were one-of-a-kind prototypes. It is still possible that one or more examples of these may yet be unearthed, but as the war ended 65 years ago, the chances of such events happening are steadily approaching zero.

The following list shows the type, popular name and the approximate number built, though such numbers for some countries (notably the USSR) are impossible to find with any degree of certainty.

Fighters

Unites States

Type	Number
Republic P-43 Lancer	258
Curtiss P-46	2
Lockheed P-49	1
Grumman P-50	1
Vultee P-54	2
Lockheed P-58 Chain Lightning	1
Curtiss P-60	?
Curtiss P-62	1
Vultee P-66 Vanguard	144
McDonnell P-67	1
Republic P-72	2
Bell P-77	2
Northrop P-79	?
Bell P-83	1
Bell FL-1 Airabonita	1
Boeing F8B	3
Curtiss F14C	1
Grumman F5F Skyrocket	?
Curtiss-Wright CW-21 Demon	24

Great Britain

Type	Number
Blackburn Roc	136
Blackburn Firebrand	39
de Havilland 103 Hornet	62
Gloster F.9/37	2
Hawker Tornado	4
Martin-Baker MB.3	1
Martin-Baker MB.5	1
Miles M.20	2
Vickers 432	1
Westland Whirlwind	112
Westland Welkin	68

France

Type	Number
Arsenal VG-30 series	17
Arsenal-Delanne 10	1
Bleriot S.510	?

Bloch MB.152	699
Bloch MB.155	32
Bloch MB.157	1
Bloch MB.700	1
CAO. 200	1
Caudron C.710	1
Caudron CR.760	2
Caudron CR.770	1
Dewoitine D.551	3
Hanriot NC-600	2
Morane-Saulnier M.S.440	?
Morane-Saulnier M.S.450	3
Potez 63	?
Potez 230	1
Potez 630	81
Potez 631	190
Potez 670	1
Roussel 30	1
SNCAO. 200	?
Sud-Est SE.100	2

Belgium

Renard R38	1
Renard R40	1

Netherlands

De Schelde S.21	1
Fokker D.XXIII	1
Koolhoven F.K.58	20

Czechoslovakia

Avia Av.135	?

Poland

PZL P.24	109
PZL P.50 Jastrzab	1

Finland

VL Myrsky II	50

USSR

Berezniak-Isaev BI-1	1
Lavochkin LAGG-3	?
Lavochkin La-5	?
MiG-1	?
MiG-5	?
MiG-7	?
Mikoyan I-250	1
Nikitin-Sevchenko IS-1	1
Polikarpov I-17	?
Polikrpov Malyutka	1
Tikhonravov 302	1
Yatsenko I-28	2

Yugoslavia

Ikarus IK2	14
Rogozarski IK3	54

Germany

Blohm & Voss BV 40	6
Heinkel He 100	20
Heinkel He 112	66
Focke Wulf FW 154 Moskito	30
Focke Wulf FW 159	?
Focke Wulf FW 187	?
Arado Ar 240	14

Heinkel He 280	7
Henschel Hs 129	?
Messerschmitt Me 328	?
Messerschmitt Me 263 (Ju 248)	1

Italy

Caproni Ca.313	?
Caproni Ca.331 Raffica	1
Caproni Ca.380 Corsaro	1
Caproni Vizzola F.4	1
Caproni Vizzola F.	15
Caproni Vizzola F.6	4+
Fiat G.56	1
IMAM Ro.57	?
IMAM Ro.58	1
Macchi C.201	1
Piaggio P.119	1
Reggiane Re.2001 Falco II	252
Reggiane Re.2005 Saggitario	49
Savioa Marchetti S.M.91	1
Savoia Marchetti S.M.92	1
S.A.I. S.S.4	1
S.A.I. 207	14
S.A.I. 403 Dardo	1

Roumania

I.A.R. 80	?

Japan

Kawasaki Ki.64 'Rob'	1
Kawasaki Ki.96	2
Kawasaki Ki.102 'Randy'	38
Kawasaki Ki.108	4
Mitsubishi A5M 'Claude'	1,000
Mitsubishi A7M 'Sam'	2
Mitsubishi Ki.83	4
Nakajima Ki.44 Shoki	1,228
Nakajima Ki.87	1
Rikugun Ki.93	2
Tachikawa Ki.94	1

Switzerland

C.3603	?

Turkey

Nuri Demirag Nu.D.36	?

Appendix B

Museums with Large Collections of World War Two Aircraft

United States

National Air & Space Museum, Washington, D.C. Main building on The Mall in the center of the city. Newer Udvar-Hazy Center annex near Dulles International Airport, 30 miles west, in Virginia. Closed 25 December. Hours: 10:00 am to 5:30 pm; summer (22 May to 7 September) Mall building open 10:00 am to 7:30 pm, Udvar-Hazy 10:00 am to 8:30 pm. No charge for admission, but $15 for car parking at Udvar-Hazy.
www.nasm.si.edu

The National Museum of the US Air Force (formerly the US Air Force Museum), north of Dayton, Ohio, on the Wright-Patterson Air Force Base. Closed Thanksgiving (4th Thursday in November), Christmas and New Year's Day. Hours: 9:00 am to 5:00 pm. No charge for admission or parking.
www.AFmuseum.com

The National Naval Aviation Museum, Pensacola Naval Air Station, Pensacola, Florida. Closed New Year's Day, Thanksgiving and Christmas. Hours: 9:00 am to 5:00 pm. No charge for admission or parking.
www.navalaviationmuseum.org

Planes of Fame, 7000 Merrill Ave., Chino Airport, Chino, California. Open from 9:00 am to 5:00 pm every day except Thanksgiving and Christmas. Planes of Fame – Grand Canyon annex museum is at the Grand Canyon-Valle Airport, Valle, Arizona. General admission – $11.00; children between 5 and 11 – $4.00.
www.planesoffame.org

Experimental Aircraft Association AirVenture Museum, Wittman Regional Airport, Oshkosh, Wisconsin. Open from 8:30 am to 5:00 pm except Sunday opening at 10:00 am. Open every day except New Year's Day, Easter Sunday, Thanksgiving and Christmas. Admission: $12.50, except seniors 62 and older $10.50, students aged 6–17 $9.50, under 6 and EAA members free.
www.airventuremuseum.org

Pima Air and Space Museum, 6000 E. Valencia Rd., Tucson, Arizona, adjacent to Davis-Monthan AFB. Open daily from 9:00 am to 5:00 pm except Thanksgiving and Christmas. Admission (June–October) $13.75 for adults 13 and older, for seniors and military $11.75, for students 7–12 $8.00. (November–May) $15.50 for adults, $12.75 for seniors and military, $9.00 for students. Five and under free.
www.pimaair.org

New England Air Museum, Bradley International Airport, Windsor Locks, Connecticut. Open daily except Thanksgiving, Christmas and New Year's Day, from 10 am to 5 pm. Admission: adults 12 and older – $10, seniors 65 and older – $9, children 4–11 – $6, 3 and under free.
www.neam.org

Fantasy of Flight, 1400 Broadway Blvd., Polk City, Florida. Open 9 am to 5 pm every day except Thanksgiving and Christmas. Admission: adults – $28.95, youths 6–15 – $14.95, 5 and under free.
www.fantasyofflight.com

Canada

Canada Aviation Museum, 11 Aviation Parkway, Ottawa, Ontario. Open every day but Christmas, and Monday–Tuesday from September through April. May through August 9 am to 5 pm; September through April 10 am to 5 pm. Admission: adults $9, students and seniors $6, ages 4–15, $5; under 4 and veterans free. www.aviationtechnomuses.ca

Europe

Great Britain

Royal Air Force Museum, Hendon, Grahame Park Way, Colindale, North London. Most halls open from 10 am to 6 pm every day except from Christmas eve through the 26th, New Year's Day and January 10–15. No charge for admission. www.rafmuseum.com

Royal Air Force Museum, Cosford, Shifnal, Shropshire. Most exhibits open every day except Christmas Eve, Christmas Day and Boxing Day (December 26), and New Year's Day, from 10 am to 6 pm. No charge for admission. www.rafmuseumcosford.org.uk

Imperial War Museum, RAF Duxford, Cambridgeshire (Junction 10 of M11 motorway). Open every day but December 24–26, between late October and mid-March from 10 am to 4 pm, otherwise 10 am to 6 pm. Admission: ages 0-to-15, free; 16–59, £16.00; 60+ and students, £12.80, disabled, £9.60. www.duxford.iwm,org.uk

Fleet Air Arm Museum, Royal Naval Air Station Yeovilton, Somerset. Open every day except December 24–26, from early April to late October, 10 am to 5:30 pm, and other times from 10 am to 4:30 pm except closed Mondays and Tuesdays. Admission: adults ages 17+, £11.00; youth 5–16, £8.00; seniors, students and veterans, £9.00. www.fleetairarm.com

Midland Air Museum, Coventry Airport, Baginton, Warwickshire. Open every day but December 25–26. April through Otober, 10 am to 5 pm, November through March, 10:30 am to 4:30 pm. Admission: adults 17+, £5.25, youth 5–16, £2.75, under 5, free, retirees and students, £4.75. www.midlandairmuseum.com

France

Musee de l'Air et de l'Espace (Air and Space Museum), le Bourget Aeroport, a few miles north of Paris. No charge for admission. Open every day but Monday; April through September, 10 am to 6 pm; October through March, 10 am to 5 pm. www.mae.org

Belgium

Brussels Air Museum, Parc du Cinquantenaire, Brussels. Open 9 am to 4:30 pm every day but Monday; closed on official public holidays. Admission free. www.airmuseum.be

Italy

Museo Storico dell'Aeronautica Militare (Italian Air Force Museum), Vigna di Valle, northwest of Rome, along Lake Garda. Open June–September from 9:30 am to 5:30 pm, and otherwise from 9:30 am to 4:30 pm, except closed on New Year's Day, Easter Sunday, Christmas and every Monday. Admission free. www.aeronautica.difesa.it

Poland

Muzeum Lotnictwa Polskiego (Polish Air Museum), east of Kracow. Open every day: Monday (for outdoor exhibits only) 9 am to 3:30 pm, free. Tuesday–Friday 9 am to 5 pm, Saturday and Sunday 10 am to 4 pm. Admission: adults – 5 zlotys, children – 3 zlotys. www.muzeumlotnictwa.pl